OXFORD WORLD'S CLASSICS

SELECTED MYTHS

PLATO (*c*.427–347 BCE), Athenian philosopher-dramatist, has had a profound and lasting influence upon Western intellectual tradition. Born into a wealthy and prominent family, he grew up during the conflict between Athens and the Peloponnesian states which engulfed the Greek world from 431 to 404 BCE. Following its turbulent aftermath, he was deeply affected by the condemnation and execution of his revered master Socrates (469–399) on charges of irreligion and corrupting the young. In revulsion from political activity, Plato devoted his life to the pursuit of philosophy and to composing memoirs of Socratic enquiry cast in dialogue form. He was strongly influenced by the Pythagorean thinkers of southern Italy and Sicily, which he is said to have visited when he was about 40. Some time after returning to Athens, he founded the Academy, an early ancestor of the modern university, devoted to philosophical and mathematical enquiry, and to the education of future rulers or 'philosopher-kings'. The Academy's most celebrated member was the young Aristotle (384–322), who studied there for the last twenty years of Plato's life. Their works mark the highest peak of philosophical achievement in antiquity, and both continue to rank among the greatest philosophers of all time.

Plato is the earliest Western philosopher from whose output complete works have been preserved. At least twenty-five of his dialogues are extant, ranging from fewer than twenty to more than three hundred pages in length. For their combination of dramatic realism, poetic beauty, intellectual vitality, and emotional power they are unique in Western literature.

CATALIN PARTENIE is a Fellow of the University of Quebec at Montreal. He has also taught at Concordia University in Montreal and held visiting research positions at the Netherlands Institute for Advanced Studies, the Hastings Center in New York, and the British School of Classical Studies at Athens, where he was an Onassis Fellow. He has translated into Romanian Plato's *Timaeus* (in collaboration), *Critias*, and *Menexenus*, and is co-editor of *Plato's Complete Works in Romanian* (Humanitas). He has also co-edited (with Tom Rockmore) *Heidegger and Plato* (Northwestern University Press).

OXFORD WORLD'S CLASSICS

*For over 100 years Oxford World's Classics have brought
readers closer to the world's great literature. Now with over 700
titles—from the 4,000-year-old myths of Mesopotamia to the
twentieth century's greatest novels—the series makes available
lesser-known as well as celebrated writing.*

*The pocket-sized hardbacks of the early years contained
introductions by Virginia Woolf, T. S. Eliot, Graham Greene,
and other literary figures which enriched the experience of reading.
Today the series is recognized for its fine scholarship and
reliability in texts that span world literature, drama and poetry,
religion, philosophy and politics. Each edition includes perceptive
commentary and essential background information to meet the
changing needs of readers.*

OXFORD WORLD'S CLASSICS

PLATO

Selected Myths

Edited by
CATALIN PARTENIE

OXFORD
UNIVERSITY PRESS

OXFORD

UNIVERSITY PRESS

Great Clarendon Street, Oxford OX2 6DP

Oxford University Press is a department of the University of Oxford.
It furthers the University's objective of excellence in research, scholarship,
and education by publishing worldwide in

Oxford New York

Auckland Bangkok Buenos Aires Cape Town Chennai
Dar es Salaam Delhi Hong Kong Istanbul Karachi Kolkata
Kuala Lumpur Madrid Melbourne Mexico City Mumbai Nairobi
São Paulo Shanghai Taipei Tokyo Toronto

Oxford is a registered trade mark of Oxford University Press
in the UK and in certain other countries

Published in the United States
by Oxford University Press Inc., New York

First published as an Oxford World's Classics paperback 2004

British Library Cataloguing in Publication Data

Data available

ISBN 0–19–280508–8

1

Typeset in Ehrhardt
by RefineCatch Limited, Bungay, Suffolk
Printed in Great Britain by
Clays Ltd., St. Ives plc

For Ioana and Luca

PREFACE

This volume brings together ten of the most celebrated Platonic myths. They belong to eight of Plato's dialogues, ranging from the early *Protagoras* and *Gorgias* to the late *Timaeus* and *Critias*. The myths appear here in the most probable chronological order of their composition. Although some of them contain deities and adapted themes of traditional Greek mythology—such as Phaethon, Zeus, the judgement after death, or the Isles of the Blessed—they may all be regarded as Plato's own inventions.

These ten myths are self-contained stories. They have journeyed through more than two thousand years like ten 'strange pilgrims' (to borrow the English title of one of García Márquez's collections of short stories), each one being always ready to seduce the reader into its enigmatic realm. They were not supposed to be assembled in a greater, coherent whole, but they bear upon many Platonic philosophical questions, and, taken as a whole, they form an unusual introduction to Plato's philosophy. The reader is invited both to contemplate their imagery and to meditate on the philosophical questions they hide in this very imagery.

Hegel claimed that 'the real value of Plato does not rest in his myths'.[1] Yet regardless of where Plato's real value lies, why would one read his myths—other than for an aesthetic reward? Plato's most famous myth is the so-called myth of the cave, from *Republic* (included here under the title 'The Cave'). In this myth men are said to be like prisoners in the heart of a deep cave. We are asked to imagine that the prisoners have their necks constrained and can look only in front of them, at some shadows projected on the wall of the cave by a fire that they cannot see. In fact, they have never seen anything but those shadows, which they believe to be real beings. At some point a prisoner manages

[1] G. W. F. Hegel, *Lectures on the History of Philosophy*, tr. E. S. Haldane, vol. i (London: Routledge & Kegan Paul, 2nd edn. 1955), 88.

to unfetter himself, and he realizes that what he believed to be real beings are mere shadows. Then a mysterious man guides him out of the cave, and the former prisoner sees that the real light is outside the cave, and that its origin is the sun. And the sun, Plato says, is an analogy for the ultimate principle of the entire existence, which he called in a previous section of *Republic* 'the good' (for more on this see the prefatory note that accompanies 'The Cave'). The myth, however, is said to be an analogy for education. Indeed, education, Plato claims, is not inserting vision into blind eyes. Rather, it is turning one's eyes from darkness to light, which involves a transformation of one's perspective on things.

Most of us would look with suspicion at a radical reading of this myth, a reading which claims that the actual aim of one's education is to grasp the ultimate principle of reality. A less radical reading, however, states that the main aim of education is to expose one to things that are outside one's purview. Most of us, I suppose, would find this reading quite appealing. We know only too well that one's immediate environment, be it popular culture or extreme specialization in an academic field, may, if not challenged by different perspectives, turn into a cave-like prison for one's mind. A less radical reading would take the myth as implying that seeing things in new perspectives is the main goal of education. Now, this is just what what Plato's myths do: they disrupt our familiarity with things and turn our eyes from what they have been accustomed to see to intriguing, unfamiliar landscapes. Their real value lies in their educative power.

Each myth here is accompanied by a short prefatory note that describes its context and points out its main philosophical aspects. The Introduction offers an overall account of Plato's use of myth, gives brief accounts of two of his main philosophical theories, the so-called theories of Forms and of Recollection (to which several myths refer), and addresses the question of why Plato used so many fictional narratives and images, even though he condemned them. It also offers a bird's-eye view of the destiny Plato's myths had in the Platonic tradition. The Introduction is jointly written by Catalin Partenie, Luc Brisson, and John Dillon (see the note on p. xiii). Three sections of the Introduction (the first section, 'Plato's Myths', and 'Why Did Plato Write Myths?') were written by Catalin Partenie and Luc Brisson: the former wrote his part in English, while the latter wrote his in French. Michael Chase translated the French text and also edited these three sections for the sake of consistency. Information on characters appearing or mentioned in the myths is to be found in the Explanatory Notes and the Index of Names.

Lesley Brown (L.B.) is the author of nine prefatory notes; Catalin Partenie (C.P.) is the author of one.

David Gallop, C. C. W. Taylor, and Robin Waterfield are the authors of the Explanatory Notes.

Texts for the Index of Names were severally contributed by David Gallop, Catalin Partenie, C. C. W. Taylor, and Robin Waterfield.

The Explanatory Notes and some entries in the Index of Names are taken from other editions of Plato's dialogues in the Oxford World's Classics series, as indicated in the Note on the Translations.

The titles of the myths are the editor's, not Plato's. For convenience, they are used throughout the volume for referring to the myths they name.

References to Plato's works are followed by the Stephanus numbers and letters; these numbers and letters, which are commonly used in scholarly references to Plato's works, refer to the pages, and their sections, of the edition by Henri Estienne (in Latin, Stephanus) of the Greek text of Plato (published in Geneva in 1578). References to the works of other ancient authors are followed by the numbers and/or letters that refer to the standard editions of these works (sometimes the name of the edition used has been indicated).

Unless otherwise noted, all quotations from Plato are taken from the volumes indicated in the Note on the Translations.

I would like to thank all the contributors for their patience and encouragement. I am especially grateful to Judith Luna, editor at

Oxford University Press, for her support and suggestions. I am also grateful to Lesley Brown and Michael Inwood for their comments on earlier drafts of this volume, and to Robin Waterfield and the copy-editor for all the improvements they suggested. Finally, I would like to express my gratitude to the University of Quebec at Montreal and its Department of Philosophy for their support.

C.P.

Montreal
April 2003

CONTENTS

ABBREVIATIONS FOR PLATO'S WORKS

Chrm.	*Charmides*
Criti.	*Critias*
Euthd.	*Euthydemus*
Grg.	*Gorgias*
L.	*Laws*
Phd.	*Phaedo*
Phdr.	*Phaedrus*
Prt.	*Protagoras*
R.	*Republic*
Sph.	*Sophist*
Stm.	*Statesman*
Smp.	*Symposium*
Ti.	*Timaeus*

INTRODUCTION

If you leaf through the newspapers nowadays you are bound to come across the word 'myth'. It usually appears in titles announcing that a widespread belief has been 'dispelled', 'nailed', 'debunked', or 'shattered' by recent research. Something that we all believed to be true—say, that lengthy holidays inspire teachers to work harder—is now contradicted by the results of a new study, and we and the media call such a popular belief, now unveiled as false, a 'myth'.

The term 'myth' is a transcription of the ancient Greek *muthos*, and this is also the case with the French *mythe*, the German *Mythos*, the Italian *mito*, and so on in most other modern European languages. But what the ancient Greeks called *muthos* was quite different from what we and the media nowadays call a 'myth'. For the ancient Greeks—at least in the archaic phase of their civilization—a myth was a story that unveiled reality, hence a true story. In archaic societies, reality was believed to be the way it is because of the way the gods brought everything into being. The primordial deeds of the gods, those that caused the world around us to be as it is, were out of our reach, for they happened at the beginning of time. But they have been preserved in words, in stories that can make us witness them anew. These stories that re-create the very creation of the world by the gods, and thus unveil the ultimate origin of reality, were called by the ancient Greeks 'myths'. Between this archaic notion of myth and ours stands Plato: for him a myth is, taken as a whole, false, but there is truth in it also (cf. *R.* 377a).

The Introduction is jointly written by Catalin Partenie, Luc Brisson, and John Dillon as follows: Catalin Partenie wrote 'Plato's Life and Work', 'Myth and Philosophy', 'The Contradiction between Plato's Preaching and Practice'; Catalin Partenie and Luc Brisson wrote the first section, 'Plato's Myths', and 'Why Did Plato Write Myths?'; John Dillon wrote 'Plato's Myths in the Later Platonist Tradition'.

Plato's Life and Work

Plato was born in 427 BCE into a distinguished Athenian family. Athens, which had stood bravely against the Persian invasion of Greece, was defeated by Sparta in 404. After the war an oppressive dictatorship known as the Thirty Tyrants seized power in Athens. Although some of the Thirty Tyrants were his relatives (such as his cousin Critias: see the Index of Names) Plato refused to enter politics.

In 403 democracy was restored, and in 399 the Athenian democratic regime condemned the great philosopher Socrates to death on two fabricated charges (impiety and corruption of the youth of Athens). Plato believed that Socrates, his dear teacher, was 'the best, the wisest too, and the most just of men' (*Phd.* 118a); but the majority of Athenians were unconvinced.

After the execution of Socrates Plato travelled widely in Greece, Italy, Sicily, and possibly Egypt. In 388 he came to the court of Dionysius I of Syracuse. Dion, Dionysius' brother-in-law, was probably familiar with Plato's philosophical teachings and wanted to make him a political adviser. Plato, however, soon left Dionysius' court and returned to Athens. There, in the early fourth century, he founded the Academy, the first institution devoted to the study of philosophy. Aristotle became a student at the Academy in 367. In that same year Dionysius I died and was succeeded by Dionysius II. Dion asked Plato to come to Syracuse again, this time to look after the education of the young king. Plato came, but he soon found himself entangled in court intrigues, which finally forced Dion to leave Syracuse and Plato himself to return to Athens. In 361 Dionysius II asked Plato to come back to his court and advise him on various matters. Plato accepted but, once he arrived, he realized yet again that his advice was hardly taken into account by the king. Eventually he left Syracuse and after a dangerous voyage managed to return to Athens. In 357 Dion and his allies (among whom there were several members of Plato's Academy) attacked Dionysius II and expelled him from Syracuse; Dion was killed in 354 by his political rivals. After his third visit to Syracuse, Plato never left Athens. He died in 347.[1]

Plato wrote over twenty dialogues, whose main character is mostly Socrates. Some of the best-known dialogues are *Phaedo* (which depicts Socrates' last philosophical conversation and death), *Republic* (in which everything revolves around the political constitution of a utopian state, Callipolis, run by philosopher-kings), *Timaeus* (which offers a complex cosmological account), and *Laws* (which focuses on the legal code of Magnesia, another utopian state). There are also thirteen letters that are attributed to Plato, but their authenticity has been fiercely disputed. The *Seventh Letter*, whose authenticity has been defended by several reputable scholars, was addressed to Dion's party in Syracuse a few years after Dion's assassination, and it contains an overall account of Plato's involvement in Syracusan politics. Plato's contribution to philosophy and his constant influence on the history of philosophy, which can hardly be exaggerated, made the twentieth-century philosopher A. N. Whitehead claim that 'the safest general characterisation of the European philosophical tradition is that it consists of a series of footnotes to Plato'.[2]

Plato's Myths

There are many myths in Plato's writings. Some of them are traditional Greek myths, as found in Homer or Hesiod, though sometimes Plato slightly modifies them. Others, usually called 'Platonic myths', were invented by Plato, though some are in fact heavily modified versions of traditional Greek myths. Plato is not only a myth-teller, but also a myth-maker.

Most of the myths are narrated by Socrates. Socrates, however, attributes them to others, or introduces them as stories preserved in the memory of a given community, which transmits them

---

[1] *The Mask of Apollo* (London: Longmans, 1966), by Mary Renault, is an interesting novel about Plato's misadventures in Sicily.

[2] A. N. Whitehead, *Process and Reality: An Essay in Cosmology* (New York: Free Press, 1929), 62.

orally from one generation to another. The narration of myths was common in ancient Greek society, and Plato acknowledges this practice, mentioning its conventions either in general or in connection with the transmission of a particular myth. We learn from him that the narration of myths was often the responsibility of poets and their subordinates: rhapsodes (professional reciters of poetry), actors, and choral dancers (*R.* 373b, 377d), who performed above all in rhapsodic contests, during the great festivals (*Ti.* 21b; *Criti.* 108b, d). Rhapsodic contests took place at Athens, at the time of the Panathenaea (see the note for *Timaeus* 21a), and dramatic contests at the time of the urban Dionysia, the two great festivals of ancient Athens, in front of a socially diverse audience. The myth was composed in prose or in verse. It could be told in a recitation, with or without musical accompaniment, or in song, and its interpretation might include a choreographic arrangement. When the myth is sung, Plato claims, melody and rhythm should have no autonomy, but must illustrate the subject of the discourse (*R.* 398c–d, 399a–c; *L.* 814d–815b). Yet the myth-tellers are not necessarily poets or rhapsodes. They may be mothers (*R.* 377c, 381e; *L.* 887d), nursemaids (*R.* 377c; *L.* 887d), or old women (*Grg.* 527a; *R.* 350e); their audience was much more limited, and consisted essentially of children younger than 7 years old (*R.* 377a; *L.* 887d), the age at which privileged boys in ancient Greece usually began to attend the gymnasium (a public place where exercises were practised). Children, however, are in many cases the initial addressees of myth (*R.* 377a–b; *Stm.* 268e).

Whether invented by him or not, for Plato a myth is a story dealing with particular beings, deeds, places, or events that are beyond our experience: the gods, the heroes, the life of the soul after death, the distant past, the creation of the world. Thus a myth is essentially unverifiable, and it can often be taken as a false discourse. Also, on various occasions, Plato contrasts mythical discourse with philosophical argument, as if this contrast represents that between irrational and rational (see, for instance, *Prt.* 324d), so we may expect that he would look at myths with legitimate suspicion. Yet Plato alludes abundantly in his work to traditional myths, adapts them, and creates new myths, to suit his purpose. What is more, he himself blurs the distinction between philosophy and mythology, as he does in *Republic* when he calls the utopian city that is at the core of *Republic*'s philosophical construction a 'myth' (376d), or in *Timaeus* when he claims that his account of the birth of the universe and man is nothing but a plausible story or myth (29d, 59c, 68d).

Both Plato's myths and his dialogues are narrative: in all of them a story is being told by a story-teller.[3] But the mythical story is different from the frame-story of the dialogues, in which two or more characters—in a particular setting and at a particular time—carry on a philosophical conversation. The mythical story is a fantastical story, for it always contains a fair amount of fantastical details. Plato is aware of that and he often makes the myth-teller admit it. In *Phaedo*, for instance, he makes Socrates say, after expounding the long myth about the afterlife, that 'to insist that those things are just as I've related them would not be fitting for a man of intelligence' (114d; see also *Phd.* 84c and *Phdr.* 265b–c). The myth, then, is not just fictional (made up), but fantastical (unrealistic), whereas the frame-story of the dialogues contains no fantastical details. This story is certainly fictional, for Plato has invented most of it, but it is a realistic fiction: apart for some incidental anachronisms, all dialogues describe realistic conversations between realistic characters in realistic settings. Thus Plato embeds philosophy-*cum*-fantastical stories into realistic stories.

Why Did Plato Write Myths?

Why did Plato season his philosophical discourse, which he sometimes refers to as *logos*, with these fantastical stories? Why

---

[3] The term 'narrative' can be construed in many ways. Here I shall use it in its standard, if restrictive, meaning, of which a condensed definition is given by R. Kellog and R. Scholes in their *The Nature of Narrative* (New York: Oxford University Press, 1966), 4: 'By narrative we mean all those literary works which are distinguished by two characteristics: the presence of a story and a story-teller.'

did he not avoid, as the vast majority of philosophers have done, the infiltration of *muthos* into *logos*?

First, there is a practical reason: myth is, Plato thought, an efficient means of persuasion. A myth is supposed to make one adopt a particular belief (*R.* 415c, 621c; *Phdr.* 265b; *L.* 804e, 887d, 913c, 927c), and its persuasive powers are not to be underestimated (*Phd.* 114d). The philosopher-kings who rule the ideal city imagined in *Republic* may use it as a 'noble lie' (*R.* 414b) for making the great majority of those who are not philosophers accept their places in the city, without any need for coercion. The myth of autochthony (414d–e), for instance, also mentioned in *Laws* (663d–664a), as well as the myth of metals, serves to convince the inhabitants that the city-state is one and indivisible, even though it is made up of distinct groups.[4] Or else the philosopher-kings may use myths as a way to instil in children respect for various values; and the production of myths, says Plato, should be supervised by the philosopher-kings, so that children are protected from absorbing wrong behaviour and beliefs from excessively liberal myths (*R.* 377b). A myth, however, may be useful even to a sharp-minded philosopher, for myths, at least those promoted by Plato, are supposed to make those who believe in them behave well (*Grg.* 526d–e; *Phd.* 114d; *R.* 621c).

There is, however, another reason for Plato's telling so many myths: a philosophical reason. Plato believed that humans are not able to reach the ultimate truth about reality (*R.* 517b–c; *Phdr.* 246a). As he claims in *Timaeus*, human intelligence can never be omniscient, as its model, the intelligence of the universe, is (27c–29d, 68d, 72d). A human being, he goes on in *Timaeus*, if provided with the right nurture (44b, 90c), education (44b–c, 52e, 86e, 87b), and philosophy (47b), can escape the worst of maladies—ignorance—and attain, as much as human nature permits, the truth about himself and his world (90c). But our human nature, Plato suggests by telling us so many myths, often

---

[4] In *Laws*, which depicts the legal code of a utopian city, there are plenty of references to various myths, used as preambles to introduce particular laws (see 771c, 804e, 903b, 913c, 927c, 944a).

permits us only to approximate to truth, and only indirectly, through a fictional narrative. This means that sometimes, for Plato, myth is the only device available to enable us to explore matters that are beyond our limited intellectual powers. Myth may be false in its fantastical details, but it may mirror the truth. It may, as it is said in *Republic* (377a), be false if taken as a whole, but it may lead towards truth. In short, the human mind has limitations of many sorts, so it sometimes needs myth to approximate to the truth about what lies beyond its experience.[5]

Myth and Philosophy

Four of the myths collected here—'The Judgement of Souls', 'The Other World', 'Er's Journey into the Other World', and 'The Winged Soul'—are what is usually called eschatological myths, that is, myths about the end of earthly life (from the Greek *eschaton*, 'last', 'uttermost'). In Plato, however, the end of earthly life is linked with two of his main philosophical theories: the theories of Forms and Recollection.

For Plato the human soul is immortal, and its earthly life is just one episode of its endless journey through time. 'The Judgement of Souls' deals with the issue of immortality from an ethical perspective: after death, one's soul is going to be judged, and then punished or rewarded according to one's moral conduct in its earthly life. This eschatological scenario is reiterated in 'The Other World', the final myth of *Phaedo* (107d–108a, 113d), but there Plato refines it and gives it a distinctive Platonic touch.

---

[5] A more radical interpretation would claim that Plato's embedding philosophy-*cum*-fantastical stories into realistic stories was not supposed to mean that story-telling is an extension of philosophical discourse, but that human knowledge is fundamentally 'fictional', i.e. not entirely reliable. Yet Plato carefully crafted his dialogues so that his readers would not know whether he believed that myth is an extension of philosophical argument or an in-built dimension of human reason that cannot be left out, not even in philosophical arguments.

In *Phaedo* the soul is not only judged for its earthly life: it is also reincarnated into another body and thrown into a new earthly life, which is part of the punishment inflicted, or reward bestowed, upon it. For instance, says Plato, those 'who have cultivated gluttony, lechery, and drunkenness, and have taken no pains to avoid them, are likely to enter the forms of donkeys and animals of that sort' when reincarnated (81e). Furthermore, one's soul is now being judged both for one's moral conduct in earthly life and for the efforts one made in that life to practise real philosophy. In 'The Judgement of Souls' there is a short remark about the judgement of a philosopher's soul: such a soul, it is said there, is bound to impress Rhadamanthys, the deity who judges the souls, and be sent to the Isles of the Blessed (*Grg.* 526c). In 'The Other World' this preferential treatment of philosophers' souls is amply developed, and it is also given a philosophical grounding. Real philosophers, Plato now says, are those who strive to make dying their profession (67e) and whose lives resemble a 'cultivation of death' (81a). By that he means that a real philosopher is one who attempts to separate the soul as much as possible from the body (67c; see also 67b, 69d, 84a–b). Why? Because during its earthly life the soul has a corporeal element (81c), and the corporeal blocks the process of acquiring real knowledge, which is pure and incorporeal. 'If we're going to know anything purely, we must be rid of it [i.e. the body], and must view the objects themselves with the soul by itself' (66d–e). And why is pure knowledge not contaminated by the corporeal? Because the objects of pure knowledge, the Forms, are thoroughly incorporeal.

I am assuming, claims Plato in *Phaedo*, the existence of 'an absolute beauty and a large and all the rest' (100b). Such an absolute entity, say, absolute beauty, is called by Plato *idea* or *eidos* (cf. 102a, 103e), usually rendered in English as 'Form'. *Idea* and *eidos* are cognates of the verb *horaō*, 'to see', and they literally mean 'form' or 'shape'. Here in *Phaedo* Plato comes up with the first explicit version of his so-called theory of Forms. And what this theory claims is that (i) reality is split into two realms: that

xx

of absolute, non-perceptible, eternal Forms, and that of their perceptible, always changing embodiments; and that (ii) the Forms actually explain the way perceptible things are: a beautiful person, say, is beautiful because that person embodies the Form of beauty (in 'The Birth of Love' everything revolves around realizing that every beautiful thing is an embodiment of the Form of beauty).[6]

Now when I look at the perceptible embodiment of a Form, Plato claims, I actually recognize in it that very Form. When I look at, say, a beautiful person, I actually recognize that which makes it beautiful, namely the Form of beauty. In *Phaedo*, however, Plato takes equality, not beauty, as an example. Let us consider, he makes Socrates say there, the case of seeing equal things. 'Whenever anyone, on seeing a thing, thinks to himself, "this thing that I now see seeks to be like another reality, but falls short, and cannot be like that object: it is inferior", do we agree that the man who thinks that must previously have known the object he says it resembles but falls short of?' (74e–75a). Yes, Plato answers. 'Then it must, surely, have been before we began to see and hear and use other senses that we got knowledge of the equal itself, of what it is, if we are going to refer the equals from our sense-perceptions to it, supposing that all things are doing their best to be like it, but are inferior to it' (75b).

On my desk there are two paper-knives. I look at them and I instantly realize that these two knives are of equal length. They are equal, yet not perfectly equal. I know they are equal, however, because, Plato seems to suggest, I compare them with perfect equality, that is, with the Form of equality. If so, it is as if I instantly recognize the Form of equality in their being of an (approximate) equal length. Yet I can recognize only what I

---

[6] Plato's dialogues are usually divided into early, middle, and late. The theory of Forms is to be found, in a less articulated and refined version, in several of his early dialogues. It is, however, formally introduced in *Symposium* and *Phaedo*, which seem to be the first two of the middle dialogues. In the middle and late dialogues this theory underwent several revisions. Nevertheless, it is the most stable of Plato's theories, and throughout the middle and late dialogues he maintains these two main claims.

knew beforehand. Thus, Plato argues, I must have had previous knowledge of the Form of equality in order to recognize it in perceptible, equal things. Plato calls this act of recognizing the Form of x in an actual, perceptible x 'recollection' (73c–d, 74c–d), and his view that Forms are recognized in their perceptible embodiments is sometimes referred to as his theory of Recollection.

The Forms themselves may be embodied by perceptible objects, but they are pure, unaffected by their own embodiments, and their knowledge must also be so: pure, non-perceptible, not contaminated by anything corporeal. If this is so, when did I acquire this innate, pure knowledge of Forms that allows me to recollect Forms in their perceptible embodiments? Plato's answer is that this knowledge is given to us, as if our soul had acquired it before it was embodied and thrown into this earthly life. If knowledge is really just recollection, says Plato, then 'what we are now reminded of we must have learned at some former time. But that would be impossible, unless our souls existed somewhere before being born in this human form; so in this way too, it appears that the soul is something immortal' (72e; cf. also 75c). The pure knowledge of Forms must have been acquired when our soul was also pure, that is, before it was born into a corporeal human being (see 66e). And if our souls existed before our birth, then, Plato argues, they will continue to exist after we die (102b, 106e). To go back to the case of seeing equal things, Plato seems to say roughly this: I realize that two perceptible objects are of equal length, yet not perfectly equal; I know they are equal because I compare them with perfect equality, that is, with the Form of equality, which I cannot have come across in this life; so, I must have encountered this Form in a previous life or interlude between lives. You may find this argument implausible, but Plato seems to have taken it quite seriously. He would not insist that all its details are true (see *Phd.* 114d), but would claim that the existence of Forms calls for postulating an innate knowledge of them, and that an innate knowledge of Forms calls for postulating the soul's immortality and reincarnations (see 92d).[7]

At least three of the eschatological myths collected here—'The Other World', 'Er's Journey into the Other World', and 'The Winged Soul'—are intended to complement these two philosophical theories, of Forms and Recollection, by developing the narrative potential of these postulated ideas of immortality and reincarnation.

The Contradiction between Plato's Preaching and Practice

There is in Plato an inconsistency between what he says and what he does in his dialogues: on the one hand, he opposes myth to philosophical argument; but on the other, he uses myths (and other fictional narratives) abundantly, and envelops his own philosophy in fictional narrative dialogues, in what seems a schizophrenic act of sabotage. This inconsistency is linked with another, more puzzling one.

In many dialogues Plato condemns the use of images as a way of knowing things, and he contrasts any knowledge that involves images with real philosophical knowledge, which, he claims, should avoid any visual representation. In *Phaedo*, for instance, he makes Socrates say that to really know things we should not look at them with our eyes and rely on the way they appear, visually, to us. 'I was afraid', says Socrates there, 'I might be completely blinded in my soul, by looking at objects with my eyes and trying to lay hold of them with each of my senses. So I

---

[7] 'The Other World,' the final myth of *Phaedo*, embodies all these philosophical arguments into a fantastical eschatological account, and adds to them an ethical dimension. Although the soul is immortal, it is to be judged for both the moral conduct of its earthly life and the efforts it made in that life to practise real philosophy, i.e. acquire in its corporeal life as much pure knowledge as possible. 'Er's Journey into the Other World', the final myth of *Republic*, and 'The Winged Soul', the myth of *Phaedrus*, may be regarded as variations on the main themes that are at the core of the *Phaedo* myth: namely, the soul's immortality, the judgement of souls according to their moral and philosophical earthly achievements, reincarnation as part of the punishment or reward that follows judgement, the pure knowledge that the soul acquires when it is not embodied, and the forgetting of this knowledge in earthly life.

thought I should take refuge in theories, and study the truth of matters in them' (99e).

Plato's myths are full of images, ranging from complex frescos to bare sketches. Now, the image that I see when I look at the things around me, and the image I see when I listen to a myth that vividly describes, say, the geography of Tartarus, are not of the same kind. The first one is the image of real things, the second a fantasy. I acquire the first one with my eyes open, the second with my mind, and for this one I do not need to keep my eyes open; in fact, it may help if I shut them (the mind, it is said in *Symposium* (219a), begins to see clearly when the bodily eyes grow dim).[8] But even if they are of different kinds, both of them are images, and they both engage our soul on a visual track towards 'the truth of matters', which in *Phaedo* and elsewhere is contrasted with the real, non-visual, philosophical track. If so, then the opposition between myth and philosophy extends into another one—that between the visual and the philosophical approaches to things. And here, too, there is an inconsistency between what Plato says and what he does in his dialogues: on the one hand, he condemns the use of images; on the other, he uses many images and visual analogies—some of them fairly realistic, others, like those portrayed in his myths, utterly fantastical.

Plato might have said that the use of image is either part of the playfulness of philosophy (see *Phdr.* 276d, 277e), or that it is simply a good means of teaching. Plato, however, did not explain or describe this incoherence in any way. So, some scholars suggest, we have to assume that he was probably much mistaken about the method by which he reached his own philosophical

---

[8] As Plato claims in the later *Theaetetus*, we actually see *with* our soul *through* our eyes, as if they were merely instruments (184d). That is: when I see that there is something here in front of me, it is with my mind, or whatever we please to call it, that I see that there is something here in front of me. This implies that the final destination of an image is not the eye, but the mind. The mind, then, is the real screen (as it were) on which an image is projected. And if so, the image that I see when I look at the things around me, and the image I imagine when I listen to a myth, are both projected on the mind's screen.

theories.[9] This conclusion may seem fairly commonsensical. But the price for adopting it is high, for in this case we have to assume that such a careful thinker and meticulous writer as Plato failed to realize how odd this incoherence between his principles and practice about images is. Besides, this incoherence is woven together with several other, related incoherences, which can hardly be said to have escaped Plato's attention. Consider just one of them. This concerns the very names Plato uses for naming the intelligible, non-perceptible, eternal entities embodied in perceptible things, namely *idea* and *eidos*. As Plato claims in 'The Birth of Love', an *idea*, or *eidos*, say, the Form of beauty, is not perceived 'as a face or hands or any other physical feature, or as a piece of reasoning or knowledge. . . . [or] as being anywhere else either—in something like a creature or the earth or the heavens' (211a–b). No, the Form of beauty is absolute, separate, simple, and eternal (211b). But to use for these absolute entities the words *idea* and *eidos* is very puzzling indeed. As I have already mentioned, *idea* and *eidos* are cognates of the verb verb *horaō*, 'to see', and they literally mean 'outward, visual appearance', 'form', or 'shape', and both of them do occur in Plato in their, literal, visual sense (see, for instance, *Theaetetus* 157c). So why did he use precisely these words that express the visual appearance of perceptible things in order to name something that is non-visible? This is, one may argue, just a metaphor, a visual, handy metaphor. But why choose a visual metaphor for something that is claimed to be non-visible?[10]

Here is what Plato makes Socrates say in *Gorgias*: 'In my opinion it's preferable for me to be a musician with an out-of-tune lyre or a choir-leader with a cacophonous choir, and it's preferable for almost everyone in the world to find my beliefs misguided and

---

[9] See e.g. R. Robinson, *Plato's Earlier Dialectic* (2nd edn.; Oxford: Clarendon Press, 1953), 202–22.

[10] This visual metaphor is reinforced in 'The Birth of Love' by an equally awkward comparison. There Plato claims that if one eventually apprehends the Form of beauty, he does so by a sort of sight (*katopsis*, 210e, 211b, e). But why name, even if only metaphorically, a kind of knowledge that is supposed to be pure, not contaminated by any representation, a 'sight'?

wrong, rather than for just one person—me—to contradict and clash with myself' (482b–c). The contradiction between one's words and deeds was not a trivial matter for Plato. And yet in his middle and late dialogues he seems to contradict himself consciously by preaching one sort of philosophy and practising another. He must have had a serious reason for doing it. In his usual oblique manner, he must have wanted to point out something. But what? He does not say, and we can only guess. Was it meant to point out the limitations of Plato's own reason in its quest for pure knowledge? Or the limitations of human reason in general? This contradiction, however, could hardly fail to make us wonder; and Plato, like Aristotle, believed that wonder is what triggers the very act of philosophizing. Wonder, Plato says in *Theaetetus*, is actually the origin of philosophy (155d). We can only guess what this contradiction was supposed to point out. But we can be sure of what it was supposed to make us do.

Plato's Myths in the Later Platonist Tradition

Of Plato's immediate successors in the Academy, Speusippus, Xenocrates, and Heraclides of Pontus, as well as Aristotle, themselves composed dialogues as well as philosophical treatises, but we do not know that they included myths in the Platonic manner—though Heraclides composed dialogues, such as *Zoroastres* and *Abaris*, involving semi-mythical figures, and Aristotle, while composing more sober dialogues, seems to have told some interesting stories in them.[11]

---

[11] Such as that of King Midas and Silenus, in his *Eudemus*, Fr. 6 Ross. Aristotle, however, claims that 'into the subtleties of mythologists it is not worth our while to inquire seriously' (*Metaphysics* 1000a18–19). Though he admits that 'the lover of myths is in a sense a lover of wisdom, for myth is composed of wonders', and 'it is owing to their wonder that men both now and at first began to philosophize' (982b18) (translations by W. D. Ross, in J. Barnes, ed., *The Complete Works of Aristotle*, vol. ii, Princeton: Princeton University Press, 1984). As for Heraclides, we know at least that he told of a vision of one Empedotimus, probably in his work *On the Things in Hades* (Fr. 93 Wehrli), who was granted by Pluto and Persephone a view of 'the whole truth

However, none of these seems to equate to the particular way in which Plato makes use of myths as the complement for, or culmination of, lines of argument. From the later Platonist tradition also there is not much evidence of this practice being followed. The only notable exceptions are Cicero, in the mid-first century BCE, and Plutarch of Chaeronea, in the late first and early second century CE

In the case of Cicero, we have only his myth at the end of *De Republica*, the so-called 'Dream of Scipio' (VI 9–26).[12] This is, however, of great interest, as it provides a first example of the sort of eschatological myth of which Plutarch provides a number of instances. The myth is inspired, broadly, by 'The Cave', but with some influence also from 'The Other World'. What we have is a first-person narrative by Scipio Africanus the Younger, presenting a dream in which he meets his adoptive grandfather, Scipio Africanus the Elder, and then his natural father, L. Aemilius Paulus, and they take him on a guided tour of the heavenly realms, with the purpose of teaching him the true nature of the soul, and the happy destiny that awaits those, in particular, who have served their country well (not much is revealed about the fate of those who haven't!).

The metaphysics presented is actually rather peculiar, from a Platonic point of view. It is plain from Paulus' words (see 15) that the soul is to be seen as composed of the same substance as the heavenly bodies, a kind of pure fire, or ether, which is the doctrine, not of Plato, but rather of his independent-minded follower Heraclides—and possibly of Polemon, the last head of the Old Academy, as well.[13] Yet Polemon almost certainly did not compose myths, whereas Heraclides may well have, and his works

---

about souls'. This sounds interestingly similar to the contents of the myth of both Cicero and Plutarch mentioned below. Unless otherwise noted, all translations in this section are by John Dillon.

[12] This is now preserved by the late Roman writer Macrobius only in the context of his commentary upon it.

[13] See John Dillon, *The Heirs of Plato* (Oxford: Oxford University Press, 2003), ch. 4, for a defence of this position.

are perfectly well known to Cicero, so he is a more likely source of influence.

We must move on, however, about a hundred and fifty years, from Cicero to Plutarch of Chaeronea, to find the only other known composer of myths within the Platonic tradition. Plutarch makes use of myths in three of his dialogues, *On the Delays in the Divine Vengeance* (*De Sera*, 563B–568A), *On the Sign of Socrates* (*De Genio*, 589F–594A), and *Concerning the Face on the Moon* (*De Facie*, 940F–945D). In each case, what we have is an eschatological myth, involving a 'heavenly ride', loosely modelled on 'The Cave', though again with influence from 'The Other World', but also embodying a considerably greater degree of 'scientific' speculation and metaphysical elaboration, developed over the intervening centuries. Plutarch is very conscious of Plato's use of myth to reinforce an argument. In the *De Facie*, for example, the myth presents a *reason* for the earth-like composition of the Moon, which has been set out 'scientifically' in the first part of the discussion. The latter part of the myth (942D onwards—the first part constitutes a most interesting frame-story, involving a tale of travel across the Atlantic) establishes the purpose of the Moon by explaining her role in the 'life-cycles' of souls. Similarly, the myth of the *De Genio* (the story of Timarchus, who has a vision of the heavens and the afterlife of the soul while incubating in the Cave of Trophonius), serves to set that inner voice of Socrates which he used to say was his guide in a more general context. Just before this myth is told (589F), one of the interlocutors, Theocritus, remarks: 'The mythical mode of discourse, too, despite the loose manner in which it does so, has a way of reaching the truth.'

Plutarch, however, is the last Platonist to attempt to emulate the Master himself in this respect. In the Neoplatonic period what we find, rather, is the determined *allegorization* of Platonic myths—a process that had probably begun as early as Numenius, in the second century CE. Plotinus himself is not much concerned with the formal exegesis of Platonic myths, but he does, in *Ennead* III 5, 'On Love', indulge in something approaching an allegorical interpretation of the tale of Poverty and Plenty in *Symposium* 203a–d. His successors, however, devoted themselves much more explicitly to such interpretation. Porphyry and Iamblichus certainly gave allegorical interpretations of the Atlantis story in *Timaeus*, and Porphyry, at least, discussed 'The Cave' (cf. Proclus, *In Platonis Rem Publicam commentarii*, II 96, 13, and *passim*).[14] The most comprehensive Neoplatonic discussion of a myth, however, is that of Proclus on 'The Cave' in the sixteenth and final essay among his *Essays on the Republic*.[15] He also treats in some detail, in his *Commentary on the Timaeus*,[16] the story of Atlantis, allegorizing it comprehensively as a struggle between opposed daemonic forces in the world, the intellectual, symbolized by Athens and the goddess Athena, and the material, symbolized by Atlantis and Poseidon.[17] We also find, in his *Platonic Theology* (book V, chs. 6 and 25), a treatment of 'The Two Cosmic Eras', allegorizing away the cosmic cycle aspect of the story, and interpreting the cycle of Cronus as a representation of the intelligible realm, in so far as it impinges upon the material world.

Other than Proclus, we have interpretations of 'The Other World' by Damascius (*In Platonis Phaedonem commentaria*, I, §§ 456–551), and of *The Judgement of Souls* by Olympiodorus (*In Platonis Gorgiam commentaria*, §§ 46–50); the former bears witness to much previous discussion of the subject, while the latter provides acute analysis of what purposes myths serve (e.g. 240, 27 ff. Westerink).

These interpretations of Platonic myths have to be seen in the context of the later Platonist belief in the divinely inspired insight, not only of Plato himself, but of a whole range of poetic, 'theological' authorities, such as Homer, Hesiod, Orpheus, and

---

[14] Proclus here describes Porphyry, at the end of a longish list of previous (Middle Platonic) interpreters, as 'the most perfect exegete of the truths hidden in the myth'.

[15] Normally misnamed his *Commentary* on that dialogue; cf. *In Platonis Rem Publicam commentarii* II 96, 1–359, 8 Kroll).

[16] Ibid., I 75, 27–195, 30.

[17] The Middle Platonist Numenius appears to have been the first to advance some version of this, ibid., I 76, 30 ff.

Musaeus, all of whom, consequently, being divinely inspired, had to be brought into agreement with one another, and with Plato, with the help of elaborate allegorization.

NOTE ON THE TRANSLATIONS

Two of the ten excerpts included in this volume are new translations, while the other eight are taken from the following editions of Plato's dialogues:

1. The Origin of Virtue (*Protagoras* 320c–323a). From *Protagoras*, translated with an Introduction and Notes by C. C. W. Taylor (Oxford: Oxford University Press, 1996).
2. The Judgement of Souls (*Gorgias* 523a–527a). From *Gorgias*, translated with an Introduction and Notes by Robin Waterfield (Oxford: Oxford University Press, 1994).
3. The Androgyne (*Symposium* 189c–193e); and
4. The Birth of Love (*Symposium* 201d–212c). From *Symposium*, translated with an Introduction and Notes by Robin Waterfield (Oxford: Oxford University Press, 1994).
5. The Other World (*Phaedo* 107c–115a). From *Phaedo*, translated with an Introduction and Notes by David Gallop (Oxford: Oxford University Press, 1993).
6. The Cave (*Republic* 514a–517a); and
7. Er's Journey into the Other World (*Republic* 614b–621d). From *Republic*, translated with an Introduction and Notes by Robin Waterfield (Oxford: Oxford University Press, 1993).
8. The Winged Soul (*Phaedrus* 246a–257a). From *Phaedrus*, translated with an Introduction and Notes by Robin Waterfield (Oxford: Oxford University Press, 2002).
9. The Two Cosmic Eras (*Statesman* 268d–274e); and
10. Atlantis and the Ancient City of Athens (*Timaeus* 20d–25d; *Critias* 108e–121c). New translations by Robin Waterfield.

With one exception, all translators have translated the Greek text of John Burnet's Oxford Classical Text, *Platonis Opera* (5 vols.; Oxford: Clarendon Press, 1900–7). The exception is *Gorgias*, whose translator has translated the Greek text of E. R. Dodds's *Plato: Gorgias* (London: Oxford University Press, 1959).

The numbers and letters which appear in the margins of the excerpts are the standard means of reference to passages in Plato's works. They refer to the pages, and their sections, of the edition by Henri Estienne (in Latin, Stephanus) of the Greek text of Plato (published in Geneva in 1578).

SELECT BIBLIOGRAPHY

The following bibliographical references list only works available in English. An extensive bibliography on Plato scholarship is available in R. Kraut, ed., *The Cambridge Companion to Plato* (Cambridge: Cambridge University Press, 1992), 493–529.

Complete Translations

Plato's complete works are now available in several editions:

The Dialogues of Plato, translated into English with analyses and introductions by B. Jowett, 4th edn., revised by order of the Jowett Copyright Trustees (Oxford: Clarendon Press, 1953).

Plato, *Complete Works*, edited with an introduction and notes by J. M. Cooper, with D. S. Hutchinson (Indianapolis: Hackett, 1997).

Plato, *The Collected Dialogues*, edited by E. Hamilton and H. Cairns (Princeton: Princeton University Press, 1989) (which includes seven dialogues in Jowett's translation).

Although no general consensus has been reached among scholars as to the chronology of Plato's works, the prevailing view is that *Protagoras, Gorgias, Symposium, Phaedo, Republic, Phaedrus, Statesman, Timaeus,* and *Critias* (from which the myths collected in this volume have been taken) were written in this order. For a brief review of the vast scholarship on the chronology of Plato's works see C. Kahn, 'Questions of Chronology', in *Plato and the Socratic Dialogue: The Philosophical Use of a Literary Form* (Cambridge: Cambridge University Press, 1998), 42–8.

Anthologies of Plato's Myths

A selection of Plato's myths is available in J. A. Stewart, *The Myths of Plato*, translated with introductory and other observations by J. A. Stewart (London and New York: Macmillan, 1905); 2nd edn. (London: Centaurus Press, 1960); 3rd edn. (New York: Barnes and Noble, 1970).

General Introductions to Plato's Philosophy

A good starting point is R. M. Hare, *Plato* (Oxford and New York: Oxford University Press, 1982). A rather brief but clear introduction to Plato's philsophy as a whole is B. Williams, *Plato* (New York: Routledge, 1999). Also very useful is R. Kraut, 'Introduction to the Study of Plato', in R. Kraut, ed., *The Cambridge Companion to Plato* (Cambridge: Cambridge University Press, 1992), 1–50. A more detailed introduction to Plato that pays special attention to Plato's literary art and his myths is R. B. Rutherford, *The Art of Plato* (Cambridge, Mass.: Harvard University Press, 1995).

Plato's Myths in General

A good short overall account of Plato's use of myth is P. Murray, 'What Is a *Muthos* for Plato?', in R. Buxton, ed., *From Myth to Reason? Studies in the Development of Greek Thought* (Oxford: Oxford University Press, 1999), 251–62.

A comprehensive treatment of the subject is Luc Brisson's *Plato the Myth Maker* [*Platon, les mots et les mythes*], translated, edited, and with an introduction by Gerard Naddaf (Chicago: University of Chicago Press, 1998). Brisson's book includes extensive bibliographical references, several indexes, and a section (135–9) that briefly discusses Marcel Detienne's influential *The Creation of Mythology* [*L'Invention de la mythologie*], translated from the French by M. Cook (Chicago: University of Chicago Press, 1986).

A valuable study of the use of myth by the Greek philosophers from Xenophanes to Plato is Kathryn A. Morgan, *Myth and Philosophy from the Pre-Socratics to Plato* (Cambridge: Cambridge University Press, 2000), which also has many references to Detienne's and Brisson's books (see above).

On the relation between *muthos* and *logos* especially useful is Christopher Rowe, 'Myth, History, and Dialectic in Plato's *Republic* and *Timaeus–Critias*', in R. Buxton, ed., *From Myth to Reason? Studies in the Development of Greek Thought* (Oxford: Oxford University Press, 1999), 251–62.

On the distinction between myth, falsehood, and fiction in Plato one can benefit by reading Christopher Gill, 'Plato on Falsehood–Not Fiction', in Christopher Gill and T. P. Wiseman, eds., *Lies and Fiction in the Ancient World* (Exeter: University of Exeter Press, 1993), 38–87.

Selected Studies on the Myths Included in this Volume

1. The Origin of Virtue (*Protagoras* 320c–323a)

O. Balaban, 'The Myth of Protagoras and Plato's Theory of Measurement', *History of Philosophy Quarterly*, 4 (1987), 371–84.

S. Kofman, 'Prometheus, the First Philosopher', *Sub-stance*, 15/50 (1986), 26–35.

H. G. Wolz, 'The Protagoras Myth and the Philosopher-Kings', *Review of Metaphysics*, 17 (1963–4), 214–34.

2. The Judgement of Souls (*Gorgias* 523a–527a)

D. L. Blank, 'The Fate of the Ignorant in Plato's *Gorgias*', *Hermes*, 119 (1991), 22–36.

Ch. B. Daniels, 'The Afterlife Myth in Plato's *Gorgias*', *Journal of Value Inquiry*, 26 (1992), 271–279.

D. Kaatmann, 'The Role of the Myth in Plato's *Gorgias*', *Dialogue* (ΦΣΤ), 38 (1995), 15–20.

3. The Androgyne (*Symposium* 189c–193e)

K. J. Dover, 'Aristophanes' Speech in Plato's *Symposium*', *Journal of Hellenic Studies*, 86 (1966), 41–50.

Ch. E. Salman, 'The Wisdom of Plato's Aristophanes', *Interpretation*, 18 (1990–1), 233–50.

A. W. Saxonhouse, 'The Net of Hephaestus: Aristophanes' Speech in the *Symposium*', *Interpretation*, 13 (1985), 15–32.

4. The Birth of Love (*Symposium* 201d–212c)

A. Bloom, 'The Ladder of Love', in Plato's *Symposium*, tr. S. Bernadete (Chicago: University of Chicago Press, 2001), 55–177.

L. Irigaray, 'Sorcerer Love: A Reading of Plato's *Symposium*, Diotima's Speech', *Hypatia*, 3 (1989), 32–44.

A. Nye, 'The Subject of Love: Diotima and Her Critics', *Journal of Value Inquiry*, 24 (1990), 135–53.

5. The Other World (*Phaedo* 107c–115a)

K. Dorter, 'The Myth of Afterlife (107c1–115a3)', in *Plato's Phaedo: An Introduction* (Toronto: Toronto University Press, 1982), 162–75.

A. Mendelson, 'Plato's *Phaedo* and the Fragility of Human Nature', *Dionysius*, 5 (1981), 29–39.

P. C. Santilli, 'Socrates and Asclepius: The Final Words', *International Studies in Philosophy*, 22 (1990), 29–39.

D. Sedley, 'Theology and Myth in the *Phaedo*', in J. J. Cleary, ed., *Boston Area Colloquium in Ancient Philosophy*, vol. v (Lanham, Md.: University of America Press, 1991), 359–83; commentary by G. Fine, 384–98.

6. The Cave (*Republic*, 514a–517a)

R. K. Elliot, 'Socrates and Plato's Cave', *Kant-Studien*, 58 (1967), 137–57.

J. Ferguson, 'Sun, Line and Cave Again', *Classical Quarterly*, 13 (1963), 188–93.

J. Malcolm, 'The Cave Revisited', *Classical Quarterly*, 31 (1981) 60–8.

C. Strang, 'Plato's Analogy of the Cave', *Oxford Studies in Ancient Philosophy*, 4 (1986), 19–34.

7. Er's Journey into the Other World (*Republic*, 614b–621d)

G. Schills, 'Plato's Myth of Er: The Light and the Spindle', *Antiquité Classique*, 62 (1993), 101–14.

I. C. Lieb, 'Philosophy as Spiritual Formation: Plato's Myth of Er', *Philosophical Quarterly*, 3 (1963), 271–85.

H. S. Thayer, 'The Myth of Er', *History of Philosophy Quarterly*, 5 (1988), 369–84.

8. The Winged Soul (*Phaedrus*, 246a–257a)

R. Bett, 'Immortality and the Nature of the Soul in the *Phaedrus*', *Phronesis*, 31 (1986), 1–26.

M. Dyson, 'Zeus and Philosophy in the Myth of Plato's *Phaedrus*', *Classical Quarterly*, 32 (1982), 307–11.

D. D. McGibbon, 'The Fall of the Soul in Plato's *Phaedrus*', *Classical Quarterly*, 14 (1964), 56–63.

M. Nussbaum, ' "This Story Isn't True": Madness, Reason, and Recantation in the *Phaedrus*', in *The Fragility of the Goodness. Luck and Ethics in Greek Tragedy and Philosophy* (Cambridge: Cambridge University Press, 1986), 200–33.

9. The Two Cosmic Eras (*Statesman* 268d–274e)

R. D. Mohr, 'The Formation of the Cosmos in the *Statesman* Myth', *Phoenix*, 32 (1978), 250–2.

A. W. Nightingale, 'Plato on the Origins of Evil: The *Statesman* Myth Reconsidered', *Ancient Philosophy*, 16 (1996), 65–91.

T. M. Robinson, 'Demiurge and World Soul in Plato's *Politicus*', *American Journal of Philosophy*, 88 (1967), 57–66.

P. Vidal-Naquet, 'Plato's Myth of the *Statesman*: The Ambiguities of the Golden Age and of History', *Journal of Hellenic Studies*, 98 (1978), 132–41.

10. Atlantis and the Ancient City of Athens (*Timaeus* 20d–25d; *Critias* 108e–121c)

C. Gill, 'The Genre of the Atlantis Story', *Classical Philology*, 72 (1977), 287–304.

—— 'Plato's Atlantis Story and the Birth of Fiction', *Philosophy and Literature*, 3 (1979), 64–78.

—— *Plato: The Atlantis Story* (Bristol: Bristol Classical Press. 1980).

K. A. Morgan, 'Designer History: Plato's Atlantis Story and Fourth-Century Ideology', *Journal of Hellenic Studies*, 118 (1998), 101–18.

G. Nadaff, 'The Atlantis Myth: An Introduction to Plato's Later Philosophy of History', *Phoenix*, 48 (1994), 189–209.

E. S. Ramage, ed., *Atlantis: Fact or Fiction?* (Bloomington: Indiana University Press, 1978).

Traditions of Platonism

For the rich and complex development of Platonism the following books by John Dillon are extremely useful: *The Golden Chain: Studies in the Development of Platonism and Christianity* (Aldershot: Gower, 1990); *The Great Tradition: Further Studies in the Development of Platonism and Early Christianity* (Aldershot: Ashgate, 1997); and *The Heirs of Plato* (Oxford: Oxford University Press, 2003). The following collection of essays is also helpful: John J. Cleary, ed., *Traditions of Platonism. Essays in Honour of John Dillon* (Aldershot: Ashgate, 1999).

Greek Mythology in General

Walter Friedrich Otto's classic study on Greek mythology and religion is particularly useful: *The Homeric Gods: The Spiritual Significance of Greek Religion* [*Die Götter Griechenlands*], translated by Moses Hadas (New York: Pantheon, 1954).

Also useful are J. P. Vernant, *The Universe, the Gods, and Men: Ancient Greek Myths* [*L'Univers, les dieux, les hommes: récits grecs des origines*], translated from the French by L. Asher (New York: HarperCollins, 2001); and P. Vidal-Naquet, *The Black Hunter: Forms of Thought and*

Forms of Society in the Greek World [*Le Chasseur noir*], translated by A. Szegedy-Maszak, with a foreword by B. Knox (Baltimore: Johns Hopkins University Press, 1986).

Myth in General

Of the vast literature on myth a very good introduction to the subject is Mircea Eliade, *Myth and Reality* [*Aspects du mythe*], translated from the French by W. R. Trask (New York and Evanston: Harper and Row, 1963); it contains a basic bibliography.

SELECTED MYTHS

1. THE ORIGIN OF VIRTUE

(*Protagoras* 320c–323a)

The dialogue *Protagoras* features a gathering of intellectuals in the house of Callias, a rich, and later notorious, Athenian. Socrates challenges the foremost professor of the group, Protagoras of Abdera, to explain to a would-be pupil what the young man would learn from studying with Protagoras. 'He'll be a better man each day he studies with me.'—'But better at what?'—'At public affairs; he'll achieve success in political debate and action.' The virtue of the citizen, then, is what Protagoras professes to teach, but Socrates wonders if it is teachable. After all, the democratic assembly at Athens recognizes experts in military and technical matters, but none, apparently, in political virtue, since all (and not a few 'experts') are allowed their say on political affairs.

The myth of the origin of virtue is the first part of Protagoras' lengthy reply. He skilfully negotiates the traps Socrates has laid for him. To defend his own profession he must argue that virtue is teachable, but he cannot risk criticizing the democratic policy of allowing everyone to speak on political affairs. His solution: to claim that virtue can be and is taught, but that in a civilized society all possess it through teaching. His myth relates how man, who missed out on endowment with natural defences such as swiftness of foot or a tough skin, was given fire and technical skill by Prometheus. But these were insufficient for man to thrive and defend himself against wild beasts as long as strife persisted between men. Only a further gift, this time from Zeus, saves man from destruction: justice (*dikē*) and conscience (*aidōs*). On Zeus' instruction his messenger Hermes gave these not just to a few but to all men; and this civic virtue, the foundation of civil society, is man's salvation (322c–d).

In the remainder of his speech Protagoras will underline the myth's meaning. Athenians are correct to regard all men as having virtue, not by nature but through teaching. Who are its teachers? All who in civil society take part in bringing up children: mothers, nurses, and neighbours. This socialization is both a product of and a prerequisite for civil society; hence in the myth it is represented as a *late* gift from Zeus, not one with which man was naturally endowed but one acquired only after a period of unsuccessful attempts to live in groups with mutual co-operation.

So Protagoras describes virtue as an induced pattern of pro-social behaviour, found widespread—though in different degrees—in society. In contrast, Socrates will go on to develop an account of virtue which makes it identical with knowledge or expertise, the knowledge which is a matter of calculation of goods and evils (equated, rather surprisingly, with pleasures and pains). Protagoras, who in his Great Speech had defended the claim that virtue is teachable, resists the account that makes it the kind of expertise described by Socrates. Socrates, who had purported to doubt that it was teachable, makes it a kind of expertise—and hence teachable—available only to a few, and desirable as a good to the possessor: a clear contrast with Protagoras' view by which virtue is widespread in society and taught by all to all precisely because 'everyone is eager to teach the next man and tell him what is right and lawful' (327b).

L.B.

———————

320c 'Once upon a time there were just the gods;* mortal beings did
d not yet exist. And when the appointed time came for them to come into being too, the gods moulded them within the earth, mixing together earth and fire and their compounds. And when they were about to bring them out into the light of day, they appointed Prometheus and Epimetheus to equip each kind with the powers it required. Epimetheus asked Prometheus to let him assign the powers himself. "Once I have assigned them," he said, "you can inspect them"; so Prometheus agreed, and
e Epimetheus assigned the powers. To some creatures he gave strength, but not speed, while he equipped the weaker with speed. He gave some claws or horns, and for those without them he devised some other power for their preservation. To those whom he made of small size, he gave winged flight, or a
321a dwelling underground; to those that he made large, he gave

their size itself as a protection. And in the same way he distributed all the other things, balancing one against another. This he did to make sure that no species should be wiped out; and when he had made them defences against mutual destruction, he devised for them protection against the elements, clothing them with thick hair and tough skins, so as to withstand cold and heat, and also to serve each kind as their own natural bedding when they lay down to sleep. And he shod b some with hooves, and others with tough, bloodless skin. Then he assigned different kinds of food to the different species; some were to live on pasture, others on the fruits of trees, others on roots, and some he made to prey on other creatures for their food. These he made less prolific, but to those on whom they preyed he gave a large increase, as a means of preserving the species.

'Now Epimetheus, not being altogether wise, didn't notice c that he had used up all the powers on the non-rational creatures; so last of all he was left with humankind, quite unprovided for, and he was at a loss what to do. As he was racking his brains Prometheus came to inspect the distribution, and saw the other creatures well provided for in every way, while man was naked and unshod, without any covering for his bed or any fangs or claws; and already the appointed day was at hand, on which man too had to come out of the earth to the light of day. Prometheus was at his wits' end to find a means of preservation for mankind, so he stole from d Hephaestus and Athena their technical skill along with the use of fire—for it was impossible for anyone to acquire or make use of that skill without fire—and that was what he gave to man. That is how man acquired his practical skill, but he did not yet have skill in running a city; Zeus kept watch over that. Prometheus had no time to penetrate the citadel of Zeus— moreover the guards of Zeus were terrible—but he made his way by stealth into the workshop which Athena and Hephaestus shared for the practice of their arts, and stole e Hephaestus' art of working with fire, and the other art which

322a Athena possesses,* and gave them to men. And as a result man
was well provided with resources for his life, but afterwards, so
it is said, thanks to Epimetheus, Prometheus paid the penalty
for theft.

'Since man thus shared in a divine gift, first of all through
his kinship with the gods, he was the only creature to worship
them, and he began to erect altars and images of the gods.
Then he soon developed the use of articulate speech and of
words, and discovered how to make houses and clothes and

b shoes and bedding and how to get food from the earth.* Thus
equipped, men lived at the beginning in scattered units, and
there were no cities; so they began to be destroyed by the wild
beasts, since they were altogether weaker. Their practical
art was sufficient to provide food, but insufficient for fighting
against the beasts—for they did not yet possess the art of
running a city, of which the art of warfare is part—and so
they sought to come together and save themselves by founding
cities. Now when they came together, they treated each other
with injustice, not possessing the art of running a city, so
they scattered and began to be destroyed once again. So

c Zeus, fearing that our race would be wholly wiped out, sent
Hermes bringing conscience and justice to mankind, to be the
principles of organization of cities and the bonds of friendship. Now Hermes asked Zeus about the manner in which he
was to give conscience and justice to men: "Shall I distribute
these in the same way as the arts? These are distributed thus:
one doctor is sufficient for many laymen, and so with the other
experts. Shall I give justice and conscience to men in that way
too, or distribute them to all?"

d   '"To all," said Zeus, "and let all share in them; for cities
could not come into being, if only a few shared in them as in
the other arts. And lay down on my authority a law that he who
cannot share in conscience and justice is to be killed as a plague
on the city." So that, Socrates, is why when there is a question
about how to do well in carpentry or any other expertise,
everyone including the Athenians thinks it right that only a

6

few should give advice, and won't put up with advice from anyone else, as you say—and quite right, too, in my view—but e when it comes to consideration of how to do well in running the city, which must proceed entirely through justice and 323a soundness of mind, they are right to accept advice from anyone, since it is incumbent on everyone to share in that sort of excellence, or else there can be no city at all.'*

2. THE JUDGEMENT OF SOULS

(*Gorgias* 523a–527a)

The myth of judgement which closes *Gorgias* is told by Socrates to
Callicles, an outspoken defender of immorality, and an inspiration
for Nietzsche's 'revaluation of values'. Socrates has argued with
increasing passion and vigour against the value of rhetoric, the art
of speaking well in public, in the face of its proponents, the sophists
Gorgias and Polus, and the aristocratic Callicles. Socrates insisted
that it is not being skilled in rhetoric, but being just and avoiding
wickedness, which offers the surest route to personal happiness
and well-being. From Polus, who agreed that a life of injustice
is disgraceful but reckoned it could make men such as tyrants
supremely happy, Socrates got the concession that only painful and
harmful things are disgraceful. Since injustice is not painful to the
unjust man, it must—in spite of appearances—really harm him.
Indeed, to be just is the best way of life; next best is when one
who is unjust is punished, for punishment, Socrates claims, is like
medicine: unpleasant but good for you. Worst off of all—in spite of
appearances—is the unjust man, such as the tyrant Archelaus, who
escapes punishment!

Callicles pours scorn on these claims, deriding philosophers as
pathetic characters unable to avoid shameful treatment by their
enemies. But Socrates restates his defence of justice, enunciating
the uplifting principle that what is shameful is not suffering
injustice but rather committing it. He urges Callicles to recognize
the benefits of the orderly and harmonious soul of a just person.

The concluding myth—though Socrates prefers to call it a true
logos (that is, argument)—reinforces the thesis that justice is the
sure route to happiness. Divinely appointed judges have ever sent
men, on their death, either to the Isles of the Blessed or to punishment in Tartarus. But in Cronus' time the judges made errors,
misled by outward appearances. (No doubt readers were put in
mind of Athenian courts.) To remedy this, Zeus decreed that men
should be judged naked, by naked judges; in other words, the *soul*
is tested, and any scars due to unjust living are laid bare before a

judge who cannot be impressed by former wealth, station, or title. Grim punishment awaits the wicked, to benefit the curable, but, for the incurable, as a warning to others. Only a few who have lived lives beyond reproach—most likely philosophers—can hope to be judged innocent and sent to the Isles of the Blessed.

The story of eternal damnation for the unjust may indeed seem, as Socrates concedes (527a), like an old wives' tale designed to terrify children. Why did Plato choose to conclude his eloquent defence of justice with such a tale? Were the dialogue's earlier arguments for the superior happiness (in this life) of the just man not sufficient? A reader who has understood and been convinced by those arguments surely does not need, and may be repelled by, a crude promotion of justice by appeal to the torments of hell awaiting the wicked. Such a reader will recognize in the image of scars on the soul the theme that wickedness harms the individual in *this* life. The theme of eternal punishment for the incurably wicked, popular though it may have been in many religions, fits ill with Socrates' earlier arguments to show that punishment, like medicine, is designed to *benefit* the offender. The myth packs a powerful emotional punch, but it is doubtful whether it strengthens the claims of the dialogue as a whole.

L.B.

———

'Pay attention, then, as they say. It's an excellent explanation. 523a
I expect you'll think that what I'm about to tell you is just a story, but to my mind it does explain things, since it is, as far as I'm concerned, the truth.*

'As Homer records, when Zeus, Poseidon, and Pluto inherited their father's dominion, they divided it between themselves.* Now, during Cronus' reign human beings were subject to a law which the gods sanction even to this day and which is as follows: any human being who has lived a moral and god-fearing life shall on his death depart for the Isles of b the Blessed and shall dwell there, and live a trouble-free life of perfect happiness; however, anyone who has lived an immoral and godless life shall be imprisoned in the place of retribution and justice, which is called Tartarus.* In the time of Cronus, and in the relatively recent past during Zeus' reign as well, living judges dealt with living people and passed judgement upon them on the day of their impending death, which made the administration of justice poor. So Pluto and the supervisors of the Isles of the Blessed came and told Zeus that the wrong kinds of people were getting through to both places.

c   'So Zeus said, "I'll put an end to that. The reason the administration of justice is poor at the moment is that people are being assessed with their clothes on, in the sense that they come before the court during their lifetimes, and plenty of people with corrupt souls are dressed in attractive bodies, noble birth, and wealth; also, when it's their turn to be judged, a lot of witnesses come forward and testify to the exemplary

d lives these people have led. All this impresses the judges. Besides, the judges themselves are wearing clothes as well: their souls are enclosed within eyes and ears and bodies in general. All this—their own clothing and that of the people they're assessing—constitutes a barrier. The first job", he went on, "is to stop people knowing in advance when they're going to die, as they do at the moment. Prometheus has already

e been told to put an end to this, in fact. Second, they'd better be judged naked, stripped of all this clothing—in other words, they have to be judged after they've died. If the assessment is to be fair, the judge had better be naked as well—which is to say, dead—so that with an unhampered soul he can scrutinize the unhampered soul of a freshly dead individual who isn't surrounded by his friends and relatives, and has left all those trappings behind in the world. As a matter of fact, I realized what was going on before you did, and I made three of my sons judges—Minos and Rhadamanthys from Asia, and

524a Aeacus from Europe. After their death, they'll set up court in the meadow, at the junction where the two roads branch off towards the Isles of the Blessed and Tartarus respectively.* Rhadamanthys will judge those who have come from Asia, Aeacus those from Europe;* but I'll give Minos the privilege of making a final decision if the other two are ever at a loss. In this way, the decision about which road people are to take will be as fair as possible."

'That's the explanation I've heard, Callicles, and I'm convinced of its truth. What are its implications? The ones I can b see are as follows. It seems to me that death turns out to be nothing but the separation from each other of two things, the soul and the body. Now, once they have been separated, each of them remains in more or less the same state as it was when the person was alive. It isn't just the body which displays its innate features and the attributes it gained as a result of treatment it received and things which happened to it. For instance, big c people (whether their build was due to nature or nurture or both) make big corpses once they're dead, fat people make fat corpses, and so on; anyone who wore his hair long will have a long-haired corpse; if he was a felon, with his body scarred and marked by all the floggings and other injuries he received while he was alive, his body is going to show these marks after his death as well; any broken or deformed limbs a person had during his lifetime will be visible in exactly the same state after he's dead as well. In a word, all or most of the physical d attributes a person has during his lifetime also remain visible for a while after his death.

'Well, Callicles, I think the same goes for the soul too. Once the soul has been stripped of the body, all its features become obvious—its innate features and also the attributes the person has lodged in his soul through his behaviour in particular situations. So when people come before their judge, as Asians do before Rhadamanthys, for instance, then Rhadamanthys e makes them stand there and examines their souls one by one. He doesn't know whose soul it is; in fact, he might well get hold of the soul of the king of Persia or some other king or potentate and notice that it's riddled with defects—scourged and covered in the scars which every dishonest and unjust 525a action has imprinted on it, utterly crippled by lies and arrogance and warped by a truth-free diet—and he'd also see that the promiscuity, sensuality, brutality, and self-indulgence of his behaviour have thoroughly distorted the harmony and beauty of his soul. When he sees a soul in this state, he immediately dispatches it in disgrace to prison, where it will undergo the appropriate treatment.

b   'What is appropriate? As long as the person inflicting the punishment is justified in doing so, then every instance of punishment should either help its recipient by making him a better person or should act as an example for others, in the sense that the terrifying sight of the victim's sufferings helps them to improve.* Those who are *benefited* by being punished (whether the agents of punishment are divine or human) are those whose faults are curable; nevertheless, it remains the case both here and in Hades that it takes pain and torment to produce the benefit, since that is the only way in which injustice

c can be removed. Those who act as *examples*, on the other hand, are those who have committed such awful crimes that they've become incurable. Although this means that they themselves are past help, others can be helped by watching them suffer for ever the worst, most agonizing, and most terrifying torments imaginable as a result of their sins. Their only purpose is to hang there in their prison in Hades as visible deterrents for every new criminal who arrives there.

d   'If what Polus says is true,* then in my opinion Archelaus will become one of these deterrents, and he'll be joined by anyone else who's a dictator like him. In fact, I think most of those who act as examples are drawn from the ranks of dictators, kings, potentates, and politicians, because they're the ones who can and do commit the most terrible and immoral crimes. Homer testifies to this,* since in his poems those who

e are condemned to be punished for ever in Hades are kings and potentates such as Tantalus, Sisyphus, and Tityus. However, no poet portrays Thersites (or anyone else who may have been bad, but who wasn't involved in public life) as an incurable criminal in the grip of terrible punishment, and I imagine it's because he didn't have the same scope for wrongdoing that he's better off than those who did. No, Callicles, it's power that leads men to plumb the depths of depravity. 526a

'All the same, there's nothing to stop good men gaining power too, and those who do deserve our wholehearted admiration, because it's not easy, Callicles, and therefore particularly commendable, to have so much opportunity for wrongdoing and yet to live a moral life. Few people manage it. I mean, there have been paragons like that both here in Athens and elsewhere, and I think more will appear in the future too, who practise the virtue of moral management of the affairs entrusted to them. In fact, one of them—Aristides the son b of Lysimachus—became famous throughout Greece, not just locally. But power usually corrupts people, my friend.

'Anyway, to recapitulate, when Rhadamanthys gets hold of someone like that, he doesn't even know his name or his background; all he knows is that he's a bad man. Once he's seen this about him, he puts a token* on him to indicate whether in his opinion the person is curable or incurable, and then has him led away to Tartarus, where he undergoes the appropriate treatment. Occasionally, however, he comes across a different kind of soul, one which has lived a life of moral integrity, c and which belonged to a man who played no part in public life or—and this is the most likely possibility, in my opinion, Callicles*—to a philosopher who minded his own business and remained detached from things throughout his life. When this happens, Rhadamanthys is delighted and sends him away to the Isles of the Blessed. Aeacus goes through exactly the same procedure.* Minos sits there overseeing the whole process, and while the other two each hold a staff, he alone has a golden sceptre. That's how Homer's Odysseus saw him, "with sceptre d of gold, dispensing right among the dead".*

'Well, Callicles, I myself find this account persuasive, and I intend to present the judge with as healthy a soul as possible. So I'll ignore the public honours which attract most people, follow the path of truth, and try to be as moral a person as I can during my lifetime and after my death as well. I do all I e can to recommend this course of action to others too. In particular, in response to your appeal to me, I appeal to you to take up this way of life, to engage in this struggle which, in my opinion, is as worthwhile a struggle as you'll find here in this world.* I think it's a flaw in you that you won't be able to defend yourself when the time comes for you to undergo the trial and the assessment which I've just been talking about. Instead, 527a when you come to be judged by that son of Aegina and he seizes you and takes you away, your head will spin and your mouth will gape there in that world just as much as mine would here, and the chances are that someone will smash you in the face and generally abuse you as if you were a nobody without any status at all.'

3. THE ANDROGYNE
(*Symposium* 189c–193e)

Plato's fictional account of a drinking-party, or *symposion*, is one of his liveliest works, and it has spawned, over the centuries, a host of imitations and a whole genre of sympotic literature.

An otherwise unknown Apollodorus relates, long after the supposed event, what he has heard about the sayings and doings at an aristocratic all-male drinking-party. The occasion was the first victory, at a dramatic festival, of the playwright Agathon. Exceptional not just for his writing but also for his charm and beauty, the host Agathon was the centre of attention, lionized by all but especially by his lover Pausanias—until, that is, Socrates arrives, for once not scruffy and unshod but beautifully dressed and perfumed for the occasion. Since the other revellers are suffering hangovers from the previous night, they decide to dispense with the usual drinking spree; instead they will entertain themselves by making speeches in turn in honour of Love. Other gods have received encomia by the score, but Love (or Eros) none to date. Six speeches in praise of love follow, culminating in that of Socrates, who claims he is relating the teachings of a priestess called Diotima. In the next myth, 'The Birth of Love', Diotima will pointedly correct a key theme from the speech our present myth belongs to: that made by the comic poet Aristophanes.

Trumping the previous speaker is part of the game, and Aristophanes, speaking fourth, announces that he will improve on the contributions from the doctor Eryximachus, and from Agathon's lover Pausanias. What follows is an enchanting folk-tale—comical but not laughable—akin to some of Aesop's fables, and to the myth in Protagoras' speech ('The Origin of Virtue'), in so far as it offers an aetiology, or 'how-it-came-about' story. The lifelong love and attachment of one human being to another is explained by an elaborate fantasy that present-day humans are each half of an original whole, comically described as round, eight-limbed, four-eared, and so on. These original wholes, subsequently cut in half by

Zeus to curb their ambitions, were either all-male, all-female, or 'androgyne', that is, part-man, part-woman. Once separated, the halves desire nothing other than to be reunited. Thus a present-day male will seek his counterpart, who will be male or female depending on whether the tubby, eight-limbed original of which he is a half was all-male or 'androgyne'. Similarly a woman will seek, as her lifelong partner, either a woman or a man, depending on the nature of the whole of which she was originally a half. The poignant description of a person's search to be reunited with their lost half, and the celebration in Aristophanes' narration of the unaccountable desire for lifelong union (192c–e), cannot fail to strike a chord—however anachronistically—with a modern romantic sensibility.

Earlier and later speakers at the party focus exclusively on the celebration of homosexual desire, attraction, and love, in keeping with the ethos of the *symposion* as an occasion for parading and fostering attachments between older, often married, men and young, beautiful boys. Many have doubted that the notion of sexual orientation as a fixed personality trait can be found in Greek fifth- and fourth-century society, and Aristophanes' just-so story is unusual in seeming to presuppose that an individual is, by nature, either homosexual or heterosexual, and in either case in search of a single, lifelong partner. But this is not the feature of the folk-tale singled out for comment by Socrates in the mouth of Diotima. While Aristophanes emphasizes and celebrates the particularity of love, the attachment to another whose ground is mysterious even to the lovers themselves, Diotima will insist (205d) that love must be grounded in a desire not for one's lost 'twin', but simply for the good. The need to transcend the love of particular individuals and to aspire to a love and knowledge of Beauty itself forms the second myth from *Symposium*.

L.B.

189c 'All right, then, Eryximachus,' Aristophanes said. 'Actually, I *am* planning to adopt a different approach from the one Pausanias and you took in your speeches. It seems to me that people have completely failed to appreciate how powerful Love is; otherwise, they'd have built vast temples and altars in his honour, and would have instituted enormous sacrifices. Instead, what actually happens is that he gets none of this, although he deserves more of it than any other god, since there's no god who looks out for mankind's interests more than Love. He supports us and heals precisely those ills whose d alleviation constitutes the deepest human happiness. So what I'm going to do is try to introduce you to his power, and then you can pass the message on to others.

'The starting-point is for you to understand human nature and what has happened to it.* You see, our nature wasn't originally the same as it is now: it has changed. First, there used to be three human genders, not just two—male and female—as there are nowadays. There was also a third, which was a combination of both the other two. Its name has e survived, but the gender itself has died out. In those days, there was a distinct type of androgynous person, not just the word, though like the word the gender too combined male and female; nowadays, however, only the word remains, and that counts as an insult.*

'Secondly, each person's shape was complete: people were round, with their backs and sides forming a circle.* They had four hands and the same number of legs, and two absolutely identical faces on a cylindrical neck. They had a single head 190a for their two faces (which were on opposite sides), four ears, two sets of genitals, and every other part of their bodies was how you'd imagine it on the basis of what I've said. They moved around in an upright position, as we do today, in either of their two forward directions; and when it came to running, they supported themselves on all eight of their limbs and moved rapidly round and round, just like when acrobats perform that circular manoeuvre where they stick their legs out straight and wheel over and over.

'The reason there were three genders, and the reason they were as they were, is that the original parent of the male b gender was the sun, while that of the female gender was the earth, and that of the combined gender was the moon, because the moon too is a combination, of the sun and the earth. The circularity of their shape and of their means of locomotion was due to the fact that they took after their parents.

'Now, their strength and power were terrifying, and they were also highly ambitious. They even had a go at the gods. Homer's story about how Ephialtes and Otus tried to mount
c up to heaven to attack the gods is really about them.* So Zeus and the rest of the gods met in council to try to decide what to do with them. They were in a quandary: they didn't see how they could kill them and blast them out of existence as they had the giants, because that would also do away with the veneration and sacrificial offerings the human race gave them; but they also didn't see how they could let them get away with their outrageous behaviour. After thinking long and hard about it, Zeus said, "I think I can see a way for the human race to exist, but to be weakened enough to start behaving with
d some moderation. What I'm going to do is split every single one of them into two halves; then they'll be weaker, and at the same time there'll be more in it for us because there'll be more of them. They'll walk about upright on two legs. If in our opinion they continue to behave outrageously," Zeus added, "and they refuse to settle down, I'll cut them in half again, and then they'll go hopping around on one leg."

'With these words, he cut every member of the human race in half, just as people cut sorb-apples in half when they're
e going to preserve them, or cut an egg in two with a hair.* Then he told Apollo to twist every divided person's face and half-neck round towards the gash, the idea being that the sight of their own wounds would make people behave more moderately in the future. He also told Apollo generally to heal their wounds. So Apollo twisted their heads around, and pulled the skin together from all over their bodies on to what is now called the stomach (think of purses being closed by draw-strings), leaving only a single opening in the middle of the stomach, which we call the navel, where he tied the skin up

into a knot. Then he smoothed out most of the wrinkles and
fashioned the chest with the help of a tool like the one shoe- 191a
makers use to iron out the wrinkles in leather they've got on a
last; he left a few wrinkles, however, the ones in the region
of the stomach and the navel, to act as a reminder of what
happened all that time ago.

'It was their very essence that had been split in two, so each
half missed its other half and tried to be with it; they threw
their arms around each other in an embrace and longed to be
grafted together. As a result, because they refused to do anything without their other halves, they died of starvation and b
general apathy. If one of a pair died while the other half was
left alive, the survivor went in search of another survivor to
embrace, and it didn't matter to it whether the half that it
fell in with was half of what had originally been a female whole
(it is the half, not the whole, that we nowadays call female, of
course) or of a male whole.*

'Under these circumstances, they were beginning to die out.
Zeus took pity on them, however, and came up with another
ingenious idea: he changed the position of their genitals round
to their fronts. Up until then, their genitals too had been on
the far side of their bodies, and procreation and birth hadn't
involved intercourse with one another, but with the ground,
like cicadas.* So Zeus moved their genitals round to the front c
of their bodies and thus introduced intercourse between two
human beings, with the man as the agent of generation taking
place within the woman. His reasons for doing this were to
ensure that, when couples embraced, as well as male–female
relationships leading to procreation and offspring, male–male
relationships would at least involve sexual satisfaction, so that
people would relax, get on with their work, and take care of
other aspects of life.

'So that's how, all that time ago, our innate sexual drive d
arose. Love draws our original nature back together; he tries
to reintegrate us and heal the split in our nature. Turbot-like,
each of us has been cut in half, and so we are human tallies,

constantly searching for our counterparts.* Any men who are
offcuts from the combined gender—the androgynous one, to
use its former name—are attracted to women, and therefore
most adulterers come from this group; the equivalent women
e are attracted to men and tend to become adulteresses.* Any
women who are offcuts from the female gender aren't particularly interested in men; they incline more towards women,
and therefore female homosexuals come from this group.* And
any men who are offcuts from the male gender go for males.
While they're boys, because they were sliced from the male
gender, they fall in love with men, they enjoy sex with men,
and they like to be embraced by men. These boys are the ones
192a who are outstanding in their childhood and youth, because
they're inherently more manly than others. I know they sometimes get called immoral, but that's wrong: their actions
aren't prompted by immorality, but by courage, manliness, and
masculinity. They incline towards their own characteristics
in others. There's good evidence for their quality: as adults,
they're the only men who end up in government.*

'Anyway, when they become men, they're sexually attracted
b to boys and would have nothing to do with marriage and
procreation if convention didn't override their natural
inclinations. They'd be perfectly happy to see their lives out
together without getting married. In short, then, men who are
sexually attracted to boys, and boys who love their lovers,
belong to this group and always incline towards their own
innate characteristics.

'Now, when someone who loves boys—or whatever his
sexual preferences may be—actually meets his other half, it's
an overwhelming experience. It's impossible to describe the
affection, warmth, and love they feel for each other; it's hardly
c an exaggeration to say that they don't want to spend even
a moment apart. These are the people who form unbroken
lifelong relationships together, for all that they couldn't say
what they wanted from each other. I mean, it's impossible to
believe that it's their sex-life which does this—that sex is the

reason they're each so eager and happy to be in the other's company. They obviously have some other objective, which their minds can't formulate; they only glimpse what it is and d articulate it in vague terms.

'Imagine that Hephaestus came with his tools and stood over them as they were lying together, and asked, "What is it that you humans want from each other?" And when they were unable to reply, suppose he asked instead, "Do you want to be so thoroughly together that you're never at any time apart? If that's what you want, I'd be glad to weld you together, to fuse you into a single person, instead of being two separate people, so that during your lifetime as a single person the two e of you share a single life, and then, when you die, you die as a single person, not as two separate people, and you share a single death there in Hades. Think about it: is this your hearts' desire? If this happened to you, would it bring you happiness?" It's obvious that none of them would refuse this offer; we'd find them all accepting it. There wouldn't be the slightest doubt in any of their minds that what Hephaestus had said was what they'd been wanting all along, to be joined and fused with the one they love, to be one instead of two. And the reason for this is that originally that's exactly how we were— whole beings. "Love" is just the name we give to the desire for and pursuit of wholeness.*   193a

'As I say, in times past we were unified, but now we are scattered; Zeus punished us for our crimes in the same way as the Spartans did the Arcadians.* So the worry is that, if we fail to behave towards the gods with moderation, we'll be further divided, and in that mode of existence we'd be no different from those profiles on tombstones, sawn in two down the line of their noses. We'd be half-dice.* That's why it is everyone's duty to encourage others to behave at all times with due reverence towards the gods, since this makes it possible for good rather than bad to come our way, with Love as our leader b and commander. No one should oppose Love, and to get on the wrong side of the gods is to oppose Love. Anyone who has brought Love round to his side will find, as if by chance, the love of his life, which is a rare event at the moment.

'I don't want Eryximachus to treat my speech as a satire and imagine that I'm talking about Pausanias and Agathon. It may
c well be that they do in fact belong to that category and are both inherently masculine; but what I'm saying applies to everyone, both men and women. We human beings will never attain happiness unless we find perfect love, unless we each come across the love of our lives and thereby recover our original nature. In the context of this ideal, it necessarily follows that in our present circumstances the best thing is to get as close to the ideal as possible, and we can do this by finding the person who is our heart's delight. If we want to praise the god who is
d responsible for our finding this person, it is Love we should praise. It is Love who, for the time being, provides us with the inestimable benefit of guiding us towards our complement and, for the future, holds out the ultimate assurance—that if we conduct ourselves with due reverence towards the gods, then he will restore us to our original nature, healed and blessed with perfect happiness.

'There you are, Eryximachus,' Aristophanes said in conclusion. 'It may have been different from yours, but there's my speech on Love. As I said, I'd be grateful if you didn't try to find any humour in it, and then we can listen to all the
e remaining speakers—or rather to both of them, since only Agathon and Socrates are left.'

4. THE BIRTH OF LOVE

(*Symposium* 201d–212c)

Symposium's setting was described in the introduction to the previous myth ('The Androgyne'). That featured the fourth of the drinking-party speeches in praise of Love (the god Eros), the one given by the famous writer of comedies Aristophanes. Here we have a substantial part of what will be the sixth and last discourse on Love, that of Socrates, who typically begins by deprecating his own ability to match the others' achievements.

First Socrates gently corrects the preceding speech by Agathon, host and honorand of the party. In it Agathon had extolled Love as supremely beautiful and good among gods. But is not Love always lacking that which it loves? asks Socrates. Since what it loves is the beautiful, Love cannot itself be beautiful. Now Socrates embarks, in this fragment of *Symposium*, on what he claims is the teaching about Love of the priestess Diotima when she questioned and corrected Socrates just as he has questioned Agathon. Its opening tells a comic and surprising myth about the birth of Love. Neither beautiful nor ugly, not possessing good things but desiring them, Love is not a god but a daemon, an intermediary between gods and men.

The story of how Poverty (*Penia*) entrapped the drunken but rich and beautiful Plenty (*Poros*) into sleeping with her, an event which resulted in the birth of Love from such disparate parents, is Plato's invention. Love's parentage explains how he is both needy and resourceful in seeking to remedy the lack. As Socrates reports it, Diotima's teaching soon abandons story-telling for profound and revolutionary instruction on the true nature of Love. The true lover wants, not another person, but permanent possession of the good. To achieve this, we desire 'procreation in a beautiful medium'. Some want continuity through their children, others through fame for glorious achievements, but true loving is different from these. It is to progress from the love of persons, first their bodies and then their souls, through the love of beautiful activities and kinds of knowledge, until, leaving all these behind, the lover perceives beauty itself untrammelled by association with particular instances of beauty.

The contrast between beautiful individuals and beauty itself, together with the insistence on aspiring to an understanding of the second, presages Plato's famous theory of Forms, and his account of what true knowledge consists in (see the next two myths). But to find Diotima espousing this as the goal of *love* is remarkable. Critics are divided on the extent to which this theory of love is blind to its interpersonal nature, substituting instead an elevated but ultimately egocentric ideal of intellectual striving. Aristophanes' myth of the androgyne (see the previous myth) emphasized the particularity of love. But while Diotima's myth of Love's parentage is also designed to account for the pursuit or striving at the heart of love, the goal of her whole teaching is to play down interpersonal love, as a mere step on the ladder to the pursuit of an abstract beauty.

The solemn atmosphere engendered by the lofty teachings of the fictional priestess will soon be dissipated when the drunken Alcibiades arrives (a scene immortalized in Anselm Feuerbach's painting *Plato's Symposium*, 1869, now part of the permanent collection of Staatliche Kunsthalle, Karlsruhe); his speech, in praise not of love but of Socrates, will remind the readers of the intensity of feeling which Socrates inspired in his associates.

L.B.

———

201d 'Anyway, I'll leave you in peace now. But there's an account of Love which I heard from a woman called Diotima, who came from Mantinea and was an expert in love, as well as in a large number of other areas too. For instance, on one occasion when the Athenians performed their sacrificial rites to ward off the plague, she delayed the onset of the disease for ten years.* She also taught me the ways of love, and I'll try to repeat for you what she told me. I'll base myself on the conclusions Agathon and I reached, but I'll see if I can manage on my own now.

e 'As you explained, Agathon, it's important to start with a description of Love's nature and characteristics, before turning to what he does. I think the easiest way for me to do this is to repeat the account the woman from Mantinea once gave me in the course of a question-and-answer session we were having. I'd been saying to her, in my own words, almost exactly what Agathon was just saying to me—that Love is an important god and must be accounted attractive. She used the same arguments I used on him to prove that it actually followed from my own ideas that Love *wasn't* attractive or good.

'"What?" I exclaimed. "Do you mean to tell me, Diotima, that Love is repulsive and bad?"

'"You should be careful what you say," she replied. "Do you think that anything which isn't attractive has to be repulsive?"

'"Yes, I certainly do."

'"Do you also think that lack of knowledge is the same as ignorance? Haven't you noticed that there's middle ground between knowledge and ignorance?"

'"What middle ground?"

'"True belief," she replied. "Don't you realize that, as long as it isn't supported by a justification, true belief isn't knowledge (because you must be able to explain what you know), but isn't ignorance either (because ignorance can't have *any* involvement with the truth of things)? In fact, of course, true belief is what I said it was, an intermediate area between knowledge and ignorance."

'"You're right," I said.

'"Stop insisting, then, that 'not attractive' is the same as 'repulsive', or that 'not good' is the same as 'bad'. And then you'll also stop thinking that, just because—as you yourself have conceded—Love isn't good or attractive, he therefore has to be repulsive and bad. He might fall between these extremes."

'"Still, everyone agrees that he's an important god," I said.

'"Do you mean every expert, or are you counting non-experts too?" she asked.

'"Absolutely everyone."

'Diotima smiled and said, "But how could people who
c deny that he's even a god admit that he's an important god,
Socrates?"

'"Who are you talking about?" I asked.

'"You for one," she said, "and I'm another."

'"How can you say that?" I demanded.

'"Easily," she said, "as you'll see if you answer this
question. Don't you think that good fortune and beauty are
attributes which belong to every single god? Can you really
see yourself claiming that any god fails to be attractive and to
have an enviable life?"*

'"No, of course I wouldn't," I said.

'"And isn't it when someone has good and attractive
attributes that you call him enviable?"

'"Yes."

d '"You've admitted, however, that it's precisely because Love
lacks the qualities of goodness and attractiveness that he desires
them."

'"Yes, I have."

'"But it's inconceivable that a *god* could fail to be attractive
and good in any respect, isn't it?"

'"I suppose so."

'"Can you see now that you're one of those who don't
regard Love as a god?" she asked.

'"What is Love, then?" I asked. "Mortal?"

'"Of course not."

'"What, then?"

'"He occupies middle ground," she replied, "like those
cases we looked at earlier; he lies between mortality and
immortality."

'"And what does that make him, Diotima?"

'"An important spirit, Socrates. All spirits occupy the
e middle ground between humans and gods."

'"And what's their function?" I asked.

'"They translate and carry messages from men to gods and
from gods to men. They convey men's prayers and the gods'

26

instructions, and men's offerings and the gods' returns on these offerings. As mediators between the two, they fill the remaining space, and so make the universe an interconnected whole. They enable divination to take place and priests to perform sacrifices and rituals, cast spells, and do all kinds 203a of prophecy and sorcery. Divinity and humanity cannot meet directly; the gods only ever communicate and converse with men (in their sleep or when conscious) by means of spirits. Skill in this area is what makes a person spiritual, whereas skill in any other art or craft ties a person to the material world. There are a great many different kinds of spirits, then, and one of them is Love."

' "But who are his parents?" I asked.

' "That's rather a long story," she replied, "but I'll tell you b it all the same.* Once upon a time, the gods were celebrating the birth of Aphrodite, and among them was Plenty, whose mother was Cunning. After the feast, as you'd expect at a festive occasion, Poverty turned up to beg, so there she was by the gate. Now, Plenty had got drunk on nectar (this was before the discovery of wine) and he'd gone into Zeus' garden, collapsed, and fallen asleep. Prompted by her lack of means, Poverty came up with the idea of having a child by Plenty, so she lay with him and became pregnant with Love. The reason c Love became Aphrodite's follower and attendant, then, is that he was conceived during her birthday party; also, he is innately attracted towards beauty and Aphrodite is beautiful.

' "Now, because his parents are Plenty and Poverty, Love's situation is as follows. In the first place, he never has any money, and the usual notion that he's sensitive and attractive is quite wrong: he's a vagrant, with tough, dry skin and no shoes d on his feet.* He never has a bed to sleep on, but stretches out on the ground and sleeps in the open in doorways and by the roadside. He takes after his mother in having need as a constant companion. From his father, however, he gets his ingenuity in going after things of beauty and value, his courage, impetuosity, and energy, his skill at hunting (he's

27

constantly thinking up captivating stratagems), his desire for knowledge, his resourcefulness, his lifelong pursuit of education, and his skills with magic, herbs, and words.

e   '"He isn't essentially either immortal or mortal. Sometimes within a single day he starts by being full of life in abundance, when things are going his way, but then he dies away . . . only to take after his father and come back to life again. He has an income, but it is constantly trickling away, and consequently Love isn't ever destitute, but isn't ever well off either. He also falls between knowledge and ignorance, and 204a the reason for this is as follows. No *god* loves knowledge or desires wisdom, because gods are already wise; by the same token, no one else who is wise loves knowledge. On the other hand, ignorant people don't love knowledge or desire wisdom either, because the trouble with ignorance is precisely that if a person lacks virtue and knowledge, he's perfectly satisfied with the way he is. If a person isn't aware of a lack, he can't desire the thing which he isn't aware of lacking."*

   '"But Diotima," I said, "if it isn't either wise people or ignorant people who love wisdom, then who is it?"

b   '"Even a child would have realized by now that it is those who fall between wisdom and ignorance," Diotima said, "a category which includes Love, because knowledge is one of the most attractive things there is, and attractive things are Love's province. Love is bound, therefore, to love knowledge, and anyone who loves knowledge is bound to fall between knowledge and ignorance. Again, it's the circumstances of his birth which are responsible for this feature of his, given that his father is clever and resourceful and his mother has neither quality.

   '"There you are, then, my dear Socrates: that's what Love is like. Your conception of Love didn't surprise me at all, though. In so far as I can judge by your words, you saw Love as an object of love, rather than as a lover; that would explain why you imagined that Love was so attractive. I mean, it's true that a lovable object has to be blessed with beauty, charm, perfection, and so on, but a lover comes from a different mould, whose characteristics I've described."

'"Well, Diotima," I remarked, "I like what you're saying, but if that's what Love is like, what do we humans gain from him?"

'"That's the next point for me to try to explain, then, d Socrates," she said. "I mean, we've covered Love's nature and parentage, but there's also the fact that, according to you, he loves beauty. Suppose we were to be asked, 'Can you two tell me in what sense Love loves attractive things?' or, more clearly, 'A lover loves attractive things—but why?'"

'"Because he wants them to be his," I suggested.

'"But your answer begs another question," she pointed out. "What will a person gain if he gets these attractive things?"

'I confessed that I didn't find that a particularly easy question to answer and she went on, "Well, suppose the questioner changed tack and phrased his question in terms e of goodness instead of attractiveness. Suppose he asked, 'Now then, Socrates, a lover loves good things—but why?'"

'"He wants them to be his," I replied.

'"And what will a person gain if he gets these good things?"

'"That's a question I think I can cope with better," I said. "He'll be happy."

'"The point being that it's the possession of good things 205a that makes people happy," she said, "and there's no need for a further question about a person's reasons for wanting to be happy. Your answer seems conclusive."*

'"That's right," I said.

'"Now, do you think this desire, this love, is common to all of us? Do you think everyone wants good things to be his for ever, or do you have a different view?"

'"No," I said. "I think it's common to everyone."

'"But if everyone loves the same thing, and always does so, Socrates," she said, "why don't we describe everyone as a lover, instead of using the term selectively, for some people but b not for others?"

'"Yes, that *is* odd, isn't it?" I said.

'"Not really," she replied. "What we do, in fact, is single out a particular kind of love and apply to it the term which properly belongs to the whole range. We call *it* 'love' and use other terms for other kinds of love."

'"Can you give me an analogy?" I asked.

'"Yes, here's one. As you know, there are all kinds of creativity. It's always creativity, after all, which is responsible for something coming into existence when it didn't exist

c before. And it follows that all artefacts are actually creations or poems and that all artisans are creators or poets."*

'"Right."

'"As you also know, however," she went on, "artisans are referred to in all sorts of ways, not exclusively as poets. Just one part of the whole range of creativity, the part whose domain is music and metre, has been singled out and has gained the name of the whole range. The term 'poetry' is reserved for it alone, and it's only those with creativity in this sense who are called 'poets'."

'"You're right," I said.

d '"The same goes for love. Basically, it's always the case that the desire for good and for happiness is everyone's 'dominant, deceitful love'.* But there is a wide variety of ways of expressing this love, and those who follow other routes—for instance, business, sport, or philosophy—aren't said to be in love or to be lovers. The terminology which properly applies to the whole range is used only of those who dedicate themselves to one particular manifestation—which is called 'love' and 'being in love', while they're called 'lovers'."

'"I suppose you're right," I said.

'"Now," she continued, "what of the idea one hears that people in love are looking for their other halves?* What I'm

e suggesting, by contrast, my friend, is that love isn't a search for a half or even a whole unless the half or the whole happens to be good. I mean, we're even prepared to amputate our arms and legs if we think they're in a bad state. It's only when a person describes what he's got as good and what he hasn't got as bad that he's capable of being content with what belongs to him. In other words, the sole object of people's love is goodness. Do you agree?" 206a

' "Definitely," I said.

' "So," she said, "the simple truth of the matter is that people love goodness. Yes?"

' "Yes," I answered.

' "But hadn't we better add that they want to *get* goodness for themselves?" she asked.

' "Yes."

' "And that's not all: there's also the fact that they want goodness to be theirs *for ever*," she said.

' "Yes, we'd better add that too."

' "To sum up, then," she said, "the object of love is the permanent possession of goodness for oneself."

' "You're absolutely right," I agreed.

' "Now since this is Love's purpose in *all* his manifest- b ations," she said, "we need to ask under what conditions and in what sphere of activity the determination and energy of people with this purpose may be called love.* What does love actually do? Can you tell me?"

' "Of course not, Diotima," I said. "If I could, I wouldn't be so impressed by your knowledge. This is exactly what I come to *you* to learn about."

' "All right," she said. "I'll tell you. Love's purpose is physical and mental procreation in an attractive medium."*

' "I don't understand what you mean," I said. "I need a diviner to interpret it for me."

' "All right," she said. "I'll speak more plainly. The point c is, Socrates, that every human being is both physically and mentally pregnant. Once we reach a certain point in the prime of our lives, we instinctively desire to give birth, but we find it possible only in an attractive medium, not a repulsive one— and yes, sex between a man and a woman is a kind of birth.* It's a divine business; it is immortality in a mortal creature, this

matter of pregnancy and birth. But it can't take place where there's incompatibility, and whereas repulsiveness is incom-
d patible with anything divine, beauty is compatible with it. So Beauty plays the parts of both Fate and Eileithyia at childbirth.* That's why proximity to beauty makes a pregnant person obliging, happy, and relaxed, and so we procreate and give birth. Proximity to repulsiveness, however, makes us frown, shrink in pain, back off, and withdraw; no birth takes place, but we retain our children unborn and suffer badly. So the reason why, when pregnant and swollen, ready to burst, we get so excited in the presence of beauty is that the bearer
e of beauty releases us from our agony. You see, Socrates," she concluded, "the object of love is not beauty, as you imagine."

'"What is it, then?"

'"It is birth and procreation in a beautiful medium."*

'"All right," I said.

'"It certainly is," she said. "Why procreation? Because procreation is as close as a mortal can get to being immortal and undying. Given our agreement that the aim of love is the
207a *permanent* possession of goodness for oneself, it necessarily follows that we desire immortality along with goodness, and consequently the aim of love has to be immortality as well."*

'You can see how much I learned from what she said about the ways of love. Moreover, she once asked me, "Socrates, what do you think causes this love and desire? I mean, you can see what a terrible state animals of all kinds—beasts and birds—get into when they're seized by the desire for pro-creation. Their behaviour becomes manic under the influence
b of love. First, all they want is sex with one another, then all they want is to nurture their offspring. The weakest creatures are ready to fight even the strongest ones to the death and to sacrifice themselves for their young; they'll go to any lengths, including extreme starvation, if that's what it takes to nurture their young. If it were only human beings," she pointed out, "you might think this behaviour was based on reason; but what

causes animals to behave this way under the influence of love? Can you explain it?"   c

'When I said that I had no idea, she asked, "How do you expect to become an expert in the ways of love if you don't understand this?"

'"But that's exactly why I come to you, Diotima, as I've told you before, because I'm aware of my need for teachers. So will you explain it to me, please—and also anything else I need to know about the ways of love?"

'"Well," she said, "provided you're confident about the view we've expressed time and again about what love aims for, you shouldn't be surprised to hear that the same argument applies to animals as to humans: mortal nature does all it can to   d achieve immortality and live for ever. Its sole resource for this is the ability of reproduction constantly to replace the past generation with a new one. I mean, even during the period when any living creature is said to be a living creature and not to change . . . you know how we say that someone is the same person from childhood all the way up to old age. Although we say this, a person in fact never possesses the same attributes, but is constantly being renewed and constantly losing other qualities; this goes for his hair, flesh, bones, blood, and body in   e general. But it's not just restricted to the body: no one's mental characteristics, traits, beliefs, desires, delights, troubles, or fears ever remain the same: they come and go. But what is far more extraordinary even than this is the fact that our knowledge comes and goes as well: we gain some pieces of informa-   208a tion and lose others. The implication of this is not just that *we* don't remain the same for ever as far as our knowledge is concerned either, but that exactly the same thing happens to every single item of information. What we call 'practice', for instance, exists because knowledge leaks away. Forgetfulness is the leakage of information, and practice is the repeated renewal of vanishing information in one's memory, which preserves the knowledge. This is what makes the knowledge *appear* to be the same as before.

33

' "The point is that the continued existence of any mortal creature does not involve its remaining absolutely unchanging for all time—only gods do that. Instead, as its attributes pass

b away and age, they leave behind a new generation of attributes which resemble the old ones. This process is what enables mortal life—a body or whatever*—to share in immortality, Socrates, but immortal beings do things differently. So you shouldn't be surprised if everything instinctively values its own offspring: it is immortality which makes this devotion, which is love, a universal feature."

'In fact, I did find what she'd said surprising, so I said, "Well, you're the expert, Diotima, but is what you've been telling me really so?"

c 'She answered like a true sophist* and said, "You can be sure of it, Socrates. I mean, you can see the same principle at work in men's lives too, if you take a look at their status-seeking. You'll be surprised at your stupidity if you fail to appreciate the point of what I've been saying once you've considered how horribly people behave when they're under the influence of love of prestige and they long to 'store up fame immortal for ever'.* Look how they're even more willing to face danger for the sake of fame than they are for their children; look how

d they spend money, endure any kind of hardship, sacrifice their lives. Do you really think that Alcestis would have died for Admetus, that Achilles would have joined Patroclus in death,* or that your Athenian hero Codrus would have died in defence of his sons' kingdom, if they didn't think their courage would be remembered for ever, as in fact it is by us? No, they certainly wouldn't," she said. "I'm not sure that the prospect of undying virtue and fame of this kind isn't what motivates people to do anything, and that the better they are, the more

e this is their motivation. The point is, they're in love with immortality.

' "Now, when men are *physically* pregnant," she continued, "they're more likely to be attracted to women; their love manifests in trying to gain immortality, renown, and what they take to be happiness by producing children. Those who are *mentally* pregnant, however . . . I mean, there are people 209a whose minds are far more pregnant than their bodies; they're filled with the offspring you might expect a mind to bear and produce. What offspring? Virtue, and especially wisdom. For instance, there are the creations brought into the world by the poets and any craftsmen who count as having done original work, and then there's the most important and attractive kind of wisdom by far, the kind which enables people to manage political and domestic affairs—in other words, self-discipline and justice. And here's another case: when someone's mind has been pregnant with virtue from an early age and he's b never had a partner, then once he reaches adulthood, he longs to procreate and give birth, and so he's another one, in my opinion, who goes around searching for beauty, so that he can give birth there, since he'll never do it in an unattractive medium. Since he's pregnant, he prefers physical beauty to ugliness, and he's particularly pleased if he comes across a mind which is attractive, upright, and gifted at the same time. This is a person he immediately finds he can talk fluently to about virtue and about what qualities and practices it takes for a man to be good. In short, he takes on this person's education.* c

'"What I'm saying, in other words, is that once he's come into contact with an attractive person and become intimate with him, he produces and gives birth to the offspring he's been pregnant with for so long. He thinks of his partner all the time, whether or not he's there, and together they share in raising their offspring. Consequently, this kind of relationship involves a far stronger bond and far more constant affection than is experienced by people who are united by ordinary children, because the offspring of this relationship are particularly attractive and are closer to immortality than ordinary children.* We'd all prefer to have children of this sort rather than the human kind, and we cast envious glances at good poets like Homer and Hesiod because the kind of children they d leave behind are those which earn their parents renown and

35

'fame immortal', since the children themselves are immortal. Or what about the children Lycurgus left in Sparta who maintain the integrity of Sparta and, it's hardly going too far to say, of Greece as a whole? Then there's Solon, whom you Athenians hold in high regard as the father of your con-
e stitution. All over the world, in fact, in Greece and abroad, various men in various places have on a number of occasions engendered virtue in some form or other by creating works of beauty for public display. Quite a few of these men have even been awarded cults before now because of the immortality of their children, whereas no human child has ever yet earned his father a cult.

'"Now, it's not impossible, Socrates, that you too could be initiated into the ways of love I've spoken of so far. But I don't
210a know whether you're ready for the final grade of Watcher,* which is where even the mysteries I've spoken of lead if you go about them properly. All I can do", she said, "is tell you about them, which I'm perfectly willing to do; you must try to follow as best you can.

'"The proper way to go about this business", she said, "is for someone to start as a young man by focusing on physical beauty and initially—this depends on whether his guide* is giving him proper guidance—to love just one person's body and to give birth in that medium to beautiful reasoning. He should realize next that the beauty of any one body hardly
b differs from that of any other body, and that if it's physical beauty he's after, it's very foolish of him not to regard the beauty of all bodies as absolutely identical. Once he's realized this and so become capable of loving every single beautiful body in the world, his obsession with just one body grows less intense and strikes him as ridiculous and petty. The next stage is for him to value mental beauty so much more than physical beauty that even if someone is almost entirely lacking the bloom of youth, but still has an attractive mind, that's enough
c to kindle his love and affection, and that's all he needs to give birth to and enquire after the kinds of reasoning which help

young men's moral progress. And this in turn leaves him no choice but to look at what makes people's activities and institutions attractive and to see that here too any form of beauty is much the same as any other, so that he comes to regard physical beauty as unimportant. Then, after activities, he must press on towards the things people know, until he can see the beauty there too. Now he has beauty before his eyes in abundance, no longer a single instance of it; now the slavish d love of isolated cases of youthful beauty or human beauty of any kind is a thing of the past, as is his love of some single activity. No longer a paltry and small-minded slave, he faces instead the vast sea of beauty, and in gazing upon it his boundless love of knowledge becomes the medium in which he gives birth to plenty of beautiful, expansive reasoning and thinking, until he gains enough energy and bulk there to catch sight of a unique kind of knowledge whose natural object is the kind of beauty I will now describe.

'"Try as hard as you can to pay attention now," she said, e "because anyone who has been guided and trained in the ways of love up to this point, who has viewed things of beauty in the proper order and manner,* will now approach the culmination of love's ways and will suddenly catch sight of something of unbelievable beauty—something, Socrates, which in fact gives meaning to all his previous efforts. What he'll see is, in the first place, eternal; it doesn't come to be or cease to be, 211a and it doesn't increase or diminish. In the second place, it isn't attractive in one respect and repulsive in another, or attractive at one time but not at another, or attractive in one setting but repulsive in another, or attractive here and repulsive elsewhere, depending on how people find it. Then again, he won't perceive beauty as a face or hands or any other physical feature, or as a piece of reasoning or knowledge, and he won't perceive it as being anywhere else either—in something like a creature or the earth or the heavens. No, he'll perceive it in itself and by itself, constant and eternal, and he'll see that every other b beautiful object somehow partakes of it, but in such a way that their coming to be and ceasing to be don't increase or diminish it at all, and it remains entirely unaffected.*

'"So the right kind of love for a boy* can help you ascend from the things of this world until you begin to catch sight of *that* beauty, and then you're almost within striking distance of the goal. The proper way to go about or be guided through
c the ways of love is to start with beautiful things in this world and always make the beauty I've been talking about the reason for your ascent. You should use the things of this world as rungs in a ladder. You start by loving one attractive body and step up to two; from there you move on to physical beauty in general, from there to the beauty of people's activities, from there to the beauty of intellectual endeavours, and from there you ascend to that final intellectual endeavour,* which is no more and no less than the study of *that* beauty, so that you finally recognize true beauty.

d   '"What else could make life worth living, my dear Socrates," the woman from Mantinea said, "than seeing true beauty? If you ever do catch sight of it, gold and clothing and good-looking boys and youths will pale into insignificance beside it. At the moment, however, you get so excited by seeing an attractive boy that you want to keep him in your sight and by your side for ever, and you'd be ready—you're far from being the only one, of course—to go without food and drink, if that were possible, and to try to survive only on the sight and presence of your beloved. How do you think someone would react, then, to the sight of beauty itself, in its perfect,
e immaculate purity—not beauty tainted by human flesh and colouring and all that mortal rubbish, but absolute beauty, divine and constant? Do you think someone with his gaze fixed
212a there has a miserable life? Is that what you think about some-one who uses the appropriate faculty to see beauty and enjoy its presence? I mean, don't you appreciate that there's no other medium in which someone who uses the appropriate faculty to see beauty can give birth to true goodness instead of phantom goodness, because it is truth rather than illusion whose

company he is in? And don't you realize that the gods smile on a person who bears and nurtures true goodness and that, to the extent that any human being does, it is he who has the potential for immortality?"*

'So there you are, Phaedrus—not forgetting the rest of you. b That's what Diotima told me, and I believe her. As a believer, I try to win others as well round to the view that, in the business of acquiring immortality, it would be hard for human nature to find a better partner than Love. That's the basis of *my* claim that everyone should treat Love with reverence, and that's why I for one consider the ways of love to be very important. So I follow them exceptionally carefully myself and recommend others to do the same. It's also why, today and every day, I do all I can to praise Love's power and courage.

'That's my contribution, then, Phaedrus. You can think of it c as a eulogy of Love if you want, or you can call it whatever you like. It's up to you.'

5. THE OTHER WORLD

(*Phaedo* 107c–115a)

Phaedo relates to his friend Echecrates the events and conversations of Socrates' last day. He tells how from early morning Socrates talked with the friends who came to his prison cell, engaging in lengthy arguments about the nature of the soul, at the end of which Socrates recounted this myth. The dialogue ends with Phaedo's account of Socrates' calm and cheerful demeanour in the face of death at sunset, as he accepted the execution order and drank the appointed dose of hemlock.

Death—argues Socrates—is the parting of the soul from the body; and the philosopher must try in life to prepare himself, that is, his soul, for death, the time when the soul is freed of the encumbrances of the senses and of bodily desires, pains, and pleasures. In discussion with his friends, notably the penetrating critics Simmias and Cebes, Socrates mounts a series of arguments to show that the soul is immortal. First, he invokes a cycle of opposites, and insists that, just as waking follows falling asleep, so being reborn follows dying. Next he notes how people can gain knowledge of such things as absolute equality, though such knowledge cannot stem from empirical observation. To explain this ability, Socrates postulates that the soul can recollect knowledge which was gained in a discarnate state prior to birth—knowledge of a truer reality than the perceptible world, the so-called Forms: equality itself, beauty itself, and so forth. But though this theory of recollection may prove the prenatal existence of the soul, full immortality remains to be demonstrated. So Socrates stresses the soul's affinity to these Forms. Like the Forms, the soul is unchanging, immaterial, and indivisible; as such, it must be indestructible and hence immortal (for more on all this see the Introduction).

Midway through the discussion Socrates had already discoursed on the different fates in the afterlife of pure and impure souls. But more argument was needed to persuade his hearers that the soul really is immortal; and they are convinced by the final argument, that the soul can no more admit death than fire can admit cold or three can admit evenness. From argument Socrates now turns to narrating how different souls fare after death; but, before their various destinations are fully disclosed, he embarks on an exotic travelogue of the various regions of the earth, of which 'someone' has told him. The metaphysical thesis that true reality is other than the visible world, propounded by Socrates in his earlier arguments, is now reflected in the myth. For the story tells how the part of the earth men inhabit is but a tiny fraction of the true world; it is a mere hollow in which we are trapped, unable to see the wonders of the other world, with its marvellous colours, flowers, and dazzling gemstones. The inhabitants of this other world enjoy true happiness and communion with divinities. This image resonates with that of 'The Cave' (the next myth), especially where these inhabitants are said to see sun, moon, and stars 'as they really are'.

A quasi-scientific description of the rivers of the underworld is followed by the concluding account of the various destinies of ordinary souls, then of wicked ones—both incurable and curable—and finally of the righteous, who through their philosophic lives have earned an existence free of the body for all time, and in a place fairer even than those so far depicted. Phaedo, Simmias, and the other friends had already been convinced by the taxing arguments for the soul's immortality, so they are now suitable hearers for the story which Socrates tells. They should think it true, says Socrates, not in every detail, but in its overall theme, and recite it as a charm or spell of comfort.

L.B.

'But this much it's fair to keep in mind, friends: if a soul is 107c immortal, then it needs care, not only for the sake of this time in which what we call "life" lasts, but for the whole of time; and if anyone is going to neglect it, now the risk would seem fearful. Because if death were a separation from everything, it would be a godsend for the wicked, when they died, to be separated at once from the body and from their own wickedness along with the soul; but since, in fact, it is evidently immortal, there would

d be no other refuge from ills or salvation for it, except to become
as good and wise as possible. For the soul enters Hades taking
nothing else but its education and nurture, which are, indeed,
said to do the greatest benefit or harm to the one who has died,
at the very outset of his journey yonder.

'Now it is said that when each one has died, the spirit
allotted to each in life proceeds to bring that individual to a
certain place, where those gathered must submit to judgement,
e and then journey to Hades with the guide appointed to
conduct those in this world to the next; and when they have
experienced there the things they must, and stayed there for
the time required, another guide conveys them back here
during many long cycles of time. So the journey is not as
Aeschylus' Telephus* describes it; he says it is a simple path
108a that leads to Hades, but to me it seems to be neither simple nor
single. For then there would be no need of guides; since no
one, surely, could lose the way anywhere, if there were only
a single road. But in fact it probably has many forkings and
branchings; I speak from the evidence of the rites and observances followed here.* Now the wise and well-ordered soul
follows along, and is not unfamiliar with what befalls it; but the
soul in a state of desire for the body, as I said earlier, flutters
b around it for a long time, and around the region of the seen,
and after much resistance and many sufferings it goes along,
brought by force and against its will by the appointed spirit.
And on arriving where the others have gone, if the soul is
unpurified and has committed any such act as engaging in
wrongful killings, or performing such other deeds as may be
akin to those and the work of kindred souls, everyone shuns
and turns aside from it, and is unwilling to become its travel-
c ling companion or guide; but it wanders by itself in a state of
utter confusion, till certain periods of time have elapsed, and
when those have passed, it is taken perforce into the dwelling
meet for it; but the soul that has passed through life with
purity and moderation finds gods for travelling companions
and guides, and each inhabits the region that befits it.

'Now there are many wondrous regions in the earth, and the earth itself is of neither the nature nor the size supposed by those who usually describe it, as someone has convinced me.'

Here Simmias said: 'What do you mean by that, Socrates? d I've heard many things about the earth too, but not those that convince you; so I'd be glad to hear them.'

'Well, Simmias, I don't think the skill of Glaucus* is needed to relate what they are; although to prove them true does seem to me too hard for the skill of Glaucus—I probably couldn't do it myself, and besides, even if I knew how to, I think the life left me, Simmias, doesn't suffice for the length of the argument. e Still, nothing prevents me from telling of what I've been convinced the earth is like in shape, and of its regions.'

'Well, even that is enough,' said Simmias.

'First then, I've been convinced that if it is round and in the centre of the heaven, it needs neither air nor any other such force to prevent its falling, but the uniformity of the heaven 109a in every direction with itself is enough to support it, together with the equilibrium of the earth itself; because a thing in equilibrium placed in the middle of something uniform will be unable to incline either more or less in any direction, but being in a uniform state it will remain without incline. So that's the first thing of which I've been convinced.'

'And rightly so,' said Simmias.

'And next, that it is of vast size, and that we who dwell between the Phasis River and the Pillars of Heracles* inhabit b only a small part of it, living around the sea like ants or frogs around a marsh, and that there are many others living elsewhere in many such places. For there are many hollows all over the earth, varying in their shapes and sizes, into which water and mist and air have flowed together; and the earth itself is set in the heaven, a pure thing in pure surroundings, in which the stars are situated, and which most of those who usually describe such things name "ether";* it's from that that these c elements are the dregs, and continually flow together into the hollows of the earth. Now we ourselves are unaware that we

43

live in its hollows, and think we live above the earth—just as if someone living at the bottom of the ocean were to think he lived above the sea, and seeing the sun and the stars through the water, were to imagine that the sea was heaven, and yet

d through slowness and weakness had never reached the surface of the sea, nor emerged, stuck his head up out of the sea into this region here, and seen how much purer and fairer it really is than their world, nor had heard this from anyone else who had seen it. Now that is just what has happened to us: living in some hollow of the earth, we think we live above it, and we call the air "heaven", as if this were heaven and the stars

e moved through it; whereas the truth is just the same—because of our weakness and slowness, we are unable to pass through to the summit of the air; for were anyone to go to its surface, or gain wings and fly aloft, he would stick his head up and see— just as here the fishes of the sea stick their heads up and see the things here, so he would see the things up there; and if his nature were able to bear the vision, he would realize that that

110a is the true heaven, the genuine light, and the true earth. For this earth of ours, and its stones and all the region here, are corrupted and eaten away, as are things in the sea by the brine; nor does anything worth mentioning grow in the sea, and practically nothing is perfect, but there are eroded rocks and sand and unimaginable mud and mire, wherever there is earth as well, and things are in no way worthy to be compared with the beauties in our world. But those objects in their turn would be seen to surpass the things in our world by a far greater measure still; indeed, if it is proper to tell a tale, it's worth

b hearing, Simmias, what the things upon the earth and beneath the heaven are actually like.'

'Why yes, Socrates,' said Simmias, 'we'd be glad to hear that tale.'

'Well then, my friend, first of all the true earth, if one views it from above, is said to look like those twelve-piece leather

c balls,* variegated, a patchwork of colours, of which our colours here are, as it were, samples that painters use. There the whole

44

earth is of such colours, indeed of colours far brighter still
and purer than these: one portion is purple, marvellous for its
beauty, another is golden, and all that is white is whiter than
chalk or snow; and the earth is composed of the other colours
likewise, indeed of colours more numerous and beautiful
than any we have seen. Even its very hollows, full as they are of
water and air, give an appearance of colour, gleaming among d
the variety of the other colours, so that its general appearance
is of one continuous multi-coloured surface. That being its
nature, things that grow on it, trees and flowers and fruit, grow
in proportion; and again, the mountains contain stones likewise, whose smoothness, transparency, and beauty of colour
are in the same proportion; it is from those that the little stones
we value, sardian stones, jaspers, emeralds, and all such, are e
pieces; but there, every single one is like that, or even more
beautiful still. That is because the stones there are pure, and
not corroded or corrupted, like those here, by mildew and
brine due to the elements that have flowed together, bringing
ugliness and disease to stones and earth, and to plants and
animals as well. But the true earth is adorned with all these 111a
things, and with gold and silver also, and with the other things
of that kind as well. For they are plainly visible, being many in
number, large, and everywhere upon the earth; happy, therefore, are they who behold the sight of it. Among many other
living things upon it there are human beings, some dwelling
inland, some living by the air, as we live by the sea, and some
on islands surrounded by the air and lying close to the mainland; and in a word, what the water and the sea are to us for
our needs, the air is to them; and what air is for us, ether is b
for them. Their climate is such that they are free from sickness
and live a far longer time than people here, and they surpass us
in sight, hearing, wisdom, and all such faculties, by the extent
to which air surpasses water for its purity, and ether surpasses
air. Moreover, they have groves and temples of gods, in which
gods are truly dwellers, and utterances and prophecies, and
direct awareness of the gods; and communion of that kind they

c experience face to face. The sun and moon and stars are seen by them as they really are, and their happiness in all else accords with that.

'Such is the nature of the earth as a whole and its surroundings; but in it there are many regions within the hollows it has all around it, some deeper and some more extended than the one in which we dwell, some deeper but with a narrower
d opening than our own region, and others that are shallower in depth but broader than this one. All these are interconnected underground in every direction, by passages both narrower and wider, and they have channels through which abundant water flows from one into another, as into mixing bowls, and continuous underground rivers of unimaginable size, with waters hot and cold, and abundant fire and great rivers of fire, and many of liquid mud, some purer and some more miry, like
e the rivers of mud in Sicily that flow ahead of the lava-stream, and the lava-stream itself; with these each of the regions is filled, as the circling stream happens to reach each one on each occasion. All of this is kept moving back and forth by a kind of pulsation going on within the earth; and the nature of this pulsation is something like this: one of the openings in the
112a earth happens to be especially large, and perforated right through the earth; it is this that Homer spoke of as:

A great way off, where lies the deepest pit beneath earth;*

and it is this that he and many other poets have elsewhere called Tartarus. Now into this opening all the rivers flow together, and from it they flow out again; and each acquires its character
b from the nature of the earth through which it flows. The reason why all the streams flow out there, and flow in, is that this liquid has neither bottom nor resting place. So it pulsates and surges back and forth, and the air and the breath enveloping it do the same; because they follow it, when it rushes towards those areas of the earth and again when it returns to these; and just as in breathing the current of breath is continuously exhaled and inhaled, so there the breath pulsating

together with the liquid causes terrible and unimaginable c
winds, as it passes in and out. Now when the water recedes into
the so-called "downward" region, it flows along the courses of
those streams through the earth and fills them, as in the process of irrigation; and when it leaves there again and rushes
back here, then it fills these ones here once more; these, when
filled, flow through the channels and through the earth, and
reaching the regions into which a way has been made for each, d
they make seas and lakes and rivers and springs; and then
dipping again beneath the earth, some circling longer and
more numerous regions, and others fewer and shorter ones,
they discharge once more into Tartarus, some a long way and
others a little below where the irrigation began; but all flow in
below the point of outflow, some across from where they
poured out, and some in the same part; and there are some that
go right round in a circle, coiling once or even many times
around the earth like serpents, and then, after descending as
far as possible, discharge once more. It is possible to descend in e
either direction as far as the middle but no further; because the
part on either side slopes uphill for both sets of streams.

'Now there are many large streams of every kind; but among
their number there happen to be four in particular, the largest
of which, flowing outermost and round in a circle, is the one
called Oceanus; across from this and flowing in the opposite 113a
direction is Acheron, which flows through other desert
regions, and in particular, flowing underground, reaches the
Acherusian Lake, where the souls of most of those who have
died arrive, and where, after they have stayed for certain
appointed periods, some longer, some shorter, they are sent
forth again into the generation of living things. The third river
issues between these two, and near the point of issue it pours
into a huge region all ablaze with fire, and forms a lake larger
than our own sea, boiling with water and mud; from there it
proceeds in a circle, turbid and muddy, and coiling about b
within the earth it reaches the borders of the Acherusian Lake,
amongst other places, but does not mingle with its water; then,

after repeated coiling underground, it discharges lower down in Tartarus; that is the river they name Pyriphlegethon, and it is from this that the lava-streams blast fragments up at various points upon the earth. Across from this again issues the fourth river, first into a region terrible and wild, it is said, coloured

c bluish-grey all over, which they name the Stygian region, and the river as it discharges forms a lake, the Styx; when it has poured in there, and gained terrible powers in the water, it dips beneath the earth, coils round, and proceeds in the opposite direction to Pyriphlegethon, which it encounters in the Acherusian Lake from the opposite side; nor does the water of that river mingle with any other, but it too goes round in a circle and discharges into Tartarus opposite to Pyriphlegethon; and its name, according to the poets, is Cocytus.

d 'Such, then, is their nature. Now when those who have died arrive at the region to which the spirit conveys each one, they first submit to judgement, both those who have lived honourable and holy lives and those who have not. Those who are found to have lived indifferently journey to Acheron, embark upon certain vessels provided for them, and on these they reach the lake; there they dwell, undergoing purgation by paying the penalty for their wrongdoings, and are absolved, if any has committed any wrong, and they secure reward for their

e good deeds, each according to his desert; but all who are found to be incurable because of the magnitude of their offences, through having committed many grave acts of sacrilege, or many wrongful and illegal acts of killing, or any other deeds that may be of that sort, are hurled by the appropriate destiny into Tartarus, whence they nevermore emerge. Those, again,

114a who are found guilty of curable yet grave offences, such as an act of violence in anger against a father or a mother, and have lived the rest of their lives in penitence, or who have committed homicide in some other such fashion, must fall into Tartarus; and when they have fallen and stayed there for a year, the surge casts them forth, the homicides by way of Cocytus, and those who have assaulted father or mother by

48

way of Pyriphlegethon; then, as they are carried along and draw level with the Acherusian lake, they cry out and call, some to those they killed, others to those they injured; calling b upon them, they beg and beseech them to allow them to come forth into the lake and to receive them; and if they persuade them, they come forth and cease from their woes; but if not, they are carried back into Tartarus, and from there again into the rivers, and they do not cease from those sufferings till they persuade those they have wronged; for that is the penalty imposed upon them by their judges. But as for those who are found to have lived exceptionally holy lives, it is they who are freed and delivered from those regions within the earth, as from prisons, and who attain to the pure dwelling above, and c make their dwelling above ground. And among their number, those who have been adequately purified by philosophy live bodiless for the whole of time to come, and attain to dwelling places fairer even than those, which it is not easy to reveal, nor is the time sufficient at present. But it is for the sake of just the things we have related, Simmias, that one must do everything possible to have part in goodness and wisdom during life; for fair is the prize and great the hope.

'Now to insist that those things are just as I've related them d would not be fitting for a man of intelligence; but that either that or something like it is true about our souls and their dwellings, given that the soul evidently is immortal, that, I think, is fitting and worth risking, for one who believes that it is so—for a noble risk it is—so one should repeat such things to oneself like a spell; which is just why I've so prolonged the tale. For those reasons, then, any man should have confidence for his own soul who during his life has rejected the pleasures e of the body and its adornments as alien, thinking they do more harm than good, but has devoted himself to the pleasures of learning, and has decked his soul with no alien adornment, but 115a with its own, with temperance and justice, bravery, liberality, and truth, thus awaiting the journey he will make to Hades, whenever destiny shall summon him. Now as for you, Simmias and Cebes and the rest, you will make your several journeys at some future time, but for myself, "e'en now", as a tragic hero might say, "destiny doth summon me"; and it's just about time I made for the bath: it really seems better to take a bath before drinking the poison, and not to give the women the trouble of washing a dead body.'

6. THE CAVE

(*Republic* 514a–517a)

A paradox of *Republic* is that while it advocates a rigorous mode of dialectical thinking, devoid of images, Plato's presentation relies heavily on images, analogies, and myths. Two myths—'The Cave', and 'Er's Journey into the Other World'—are presented from *Republic*, Plato's most ambitious and most famous work. In it Socrates narrates a lengthy conversation dealing with the questions: what is justice (that is, morality) in an individual person, and who is happier, the just or the unjust person?

After an unsatisfactory exchange with the immoralist Thrasymachus, the discussion passes to the brothers Glaucon and Adeimantus who ask Socrates to investigate and to vindicate justice. In reply Socrates sketches an ideal *polis* (city), claiming that justice for such a *polis* will be analogous to, and will illuminate, justice for an individual person (or soul). Each entity, a city and an individual's soul, consists of three parts: guardians, auxiliaries, and an economic class in the *polis*; reason, spirit, and unreasoning desires in the individual. For both, justice is when each part fulfils its true function, and when the superior part—in the city, the guardians; in the individual soul, reason—rules for the good of the whole entity. The doctrine of the so-called tripartite soul has been very influential and can be seen as a precursor of Freud's psychological theories.

Can an ideal city come to be? Only, Socrates replies, if philosophers become kings or kings philosophers. The central books of *Republic* contain 'The Cave' (514a–517a), as well as the images of the sun (507a–509c) and the divided line (509d–511e) which refers to an imaginary alignment of different kinds of knowledge with their various objects. These central books determine the nature of true reality which would-be rulers must understand, and the education which will enable them to do so. A lengthy training in mathematics culminates in dialectical studies, intended to endow the would-be rulers with insight into the structure of reality, the world of the Forms, which lies behind and explains the unstable perceptible world. The highest branch of knowledge investigates the nature of the Good, but here Socrates must rely on an analogy with its 'offspring', the sun, to discuss the Good. As the sun is the source of light and is responsible for sight and for the genesis of visible things, so the Good is the source of truth and is responsible for knowledge and for the reality of that which can be known.

'The Cave' recalls the image of the sun and is a continuation of it. As Socrates explains from the outset (514a), it represents education and the lack of it (he will reiterate this point and discuss it at 518a–520d). We are to imagine men imprisoned and immobile in the depths of a long cave, facing the back wall and seeing only shadows cast by a fire behind them. Unbeknown to these prisoners, the shadows they see and the voices they hear emanate from men carrying puppet-like figures of stone and wood. In short, the prisoners take as true reality what is but a two-dimensional shadow-play cast by hidden puppets. Education is represented by the initially painful release of these prisoners (who are 'no different from us', says Socrates). When released, they are compelled to witness the realities in the cave and the even greater ones outside: first reflections, then natural phenomena, and finally stars, moon, and the sun. Here the connection with the earlier image is made explicit.

Ordinary, uneducated persons, then, suffer not from mere lack of knowledge but from pervasive and hard-to-shed illusions about what is real, and really valuable. True education requires the mind's release and turning around, and the painful shedding of the pervasive misconceptions about reality due to upbringing in 'the cave'. A third key theme of the image is found in the remarks at 517a. One who has achieved true understanding will get a harsh and uncomprehending reception from the ignorant when he tries to pass on the fruits of his enlightenment. The allusion to the condemnation and death of Socrates is unmistakable.

L.B.

514a 'Next,' I said, 'here's a situation which you can use as an analogy for the human condition—for our education or lack of it. Imagine people living in a cavernous cell down under the ground; at the far end of the cave, a long way off, there's an entrance open to the outside world. They've been there since childhood, with their legs and necks tied up in a way which keeps them in one place and allows them to look only straight b ahead, but not to turn their heads. There's firelight burning a long way further up the cave behind them, and up the slope between the fire and the prisoners there's a road, beside which you should imagine a low wall has been built—like the partition which conjurors place between themselves and their audience and above which they show their tricks.'

'All right,' he said.

'Imagine also that there are people on the other side of this wall who are carrying all sorts of artefacts. These artefacts, human statuettes, and animal models carved in stone and wood c and all kinds of materials stick out over the wall; and as you'd 515a expect, some of the people talk as they carry these objects along, while others are silent.'

'This is a strange picture you're painting,' he said, 'with strange prisoners.'

'They're no different from us,'* I said. 'I mean, in the first place, do you think they'd see anything of themselves and one another except the shadows cast by the fire on to the cave wall directly opposite them?'

'Of course not,' he said. 'They're forced to spend their lives without moving their heads.' b

'And what about the objects which were being carried along? Won't they see only their shadows as well?'

'Naturally.'

'Now, suppose they were able to talk to one another: don't you think they'd assume that their words applied to what they saw passing by in front of them?'

'They couldn't think otherwise.'

'And what if sound echoed off the prison wall opposite them? When any of the passers-by spoke, don't you think they'd be bound to assume that the sound came from a passing shadow?'

'I'm absolutely certain of it,' he said.

c 'All in all, then,' I said, 'the shadows of artefacts would con-
stitute the only reality people in this situation would
recognize.'

'That's absolutely inevitable,' he agreed.

'What do you think would happen, then,' I asked, 'if they
were set free from their bonds and cured of their inanity?*
What would it be like if they found that happening to them?
Imagine that one of them has been set free and is suddenly
made to stand up, to turn his head and walk, and to look
towards the firelight. It hurts him to do all this and he's too
dazzled to be capable of making out the objects whose shadows

d he'd formerly been looking at. And suppose someone tells him
that what he's been seeing all this time has no substance, and
that he's now closer to reality and is seeing more accurately,
because of the greater reality of the things in front of his
eyes—what do you imagine his reaction would be? And what
do you think he'd say if he were shown any of the passing
objects and had to respond to being asked what it was? Don't
you think he'd be bewildered and would think that there was
more reality in what he'd been seeing before than in what he
was being shown now?'

'Far more,' he said.

e 'And if he were forced to look at the actual firelight, don't
you think it would hurt his eyes? Don't you think he'd turn
away and run back to the things he could make out, and would
take the truth of the matter to be that these things are clearer
than what he was being shown?'

'Yes,' he agreed.

'And imagine him being dragged forcibly away from there
up the rough, steep slope,' I went on, 'without being released
until he's been pulled out into the sunlight. Wouldn't this
516a treatment cause him pain and distress? And once he's reached
the sunlight, he wouldn't be able to see a single one of the
things which are currently taken to be real, would he, because
his eyes would be overwhelmed by the sun's beams?'

'No, he wouldn't,' he answered, 'not straight away.'

'He wouldn't be able to see things up on the surface of the earth, I suppose, until he'd got used to his situation. At first, it would be shadows that he could most easily make out, then he'd move on to the reflections of people and so on in water, and later he'd be able to see the actual things themselves. Next, he'd feast his eyes on the heavenly bodies and the heavens themselves, which would be easier at night: he'd look at the light of the stars and the moon, rather than at the sun b and sunlight during the daytime.'

'Of course.'

'And at last, I imagine, he'd be able to discern and feast his eyes on the sun—not the displaced image of the sun in water or elsewhere, but the sun on its own, in its proper place.'*

'Yes, he'd inevitably come to that,' he said.

'After that, he'd start to think about the sun and he'd deduce that it is the source of the seasons and the yearly cycle, that the whole of the visible realm is its domain, and that in a sense everything which he and his peers used to see is its c responsibility.'

'Yes, that would obviously be the next point he'd come to,' he agreed.

'Now, if he recalled the cell where he'd originally lived and what passed for knowledge there and his former fellow prisoners, don't you think he'd feel happy about his own altered circumstances, and sorry for them?'

'Definitely.'

'Suppose that the prisoners used to assign prestige and credit to one another, in the sense that they rewarded speed at recognizing the shadows as they passed, and the ability to remember which ones normally come earlier and later and at the same time as which other ones, and expertise at using d this as a basis for guessing which ones would arrive next. Do you think our former prisoner would covet these honours and would envy the people who had status and power there, or would he much prefer, as Homer describes it, "being a slave labouring for someone else—someone without property",* and would put up with anything at all, in fact, rather than share their beliefs and their life?'

e   'Yes, I think he'd go through anything rather than live that way,' he said.

'Here's something else I'd like your opinion about,' I said. 'If he went back underground and sat down again in the same spot, wouldn't the sudden transition from the sunlight mean that his eyes would be overwhelmed by darkness?'

'Certainly,' he replied.

'Now, the process of adjustment would be quite long this time, and suppose that before his eyes had settled down and

517a while he wasn't seeing well, he had once again to compete against those same old prisoners at identifying those shadows. Wouldn't he make a fool of himself? Wouldn't they say that he'd come back from his upward journey with his eyes ruined, and that it wasn't even worth trying to go up there? And wouldn't they—if they could—grab hold of anyone who tried to set them free and take them up there, and kill him?'*

'They certainly would,' he said.

7. ER'S JOURNEY INTO
THE OTHER WORLD

(*Republic* 614b–621d)

Plato's *Republic* ends with the myth of Er. It relates how the soldier Er, apparently killed on the battlefield, visits the underworld but is allowed to return to earth to report what he saw. Judges below assign rewards and punishments to the newly dead, sending them up to heaven or down to hell, according to desert. Other souls are returning to the field of judgement after a millennium of reward or punishment; Er journeys with them to a new place to view the wonders of the cosmos, represented as a giant spindle in the lap of the goddess Necessity. Ready for reincarnation, these souls select a new life, human or animal, from among a limited number of choices and in the order assigned to each by lot. How they choose depends on these but also on what lessons they have learned from their previous lives and the rewards or punishments just enjoyed or endured.

The avowed purpose of the myth (614a) is to fill out the account of the benefits an individual gains from being just. Socrates had undertaken (book 2) to show that a just life is better for a person than an unjust one, no matter what the just person may suffer. To do so he explained how justice for an individual is a matter of the harmony of the three parts of the soul; such harmony is desirable in itself and makes the individual happier than any unjust person. At 612a–b he reminds the listeners that until now he has kept the promise to focus on justice itself and ignore the rewards accruing to a just person from men and gods. Now he gets their permission to include an account of such rewards, especially those awaiting the just soul after death.

But Er's story contains far more than an account of divine judgement, rewards, and punishments. The further elements have many resonances with what has come before in *Republic*. First, the theme of harmony. The order of the cosmic elements and the vocal harmony produced by the Sirens, each appointed to one of the rotating heavenly circles, recall the emphasis on justice, in both the

57

soul and the city, as a harmony of the constituent parts. Indeed the order and concentric arrangement of the cosmic entities as described in the myth recalls the order and interconnection of the Forms which books 6 and 7 describe as the objects of philosophical study.

Another recurring theme is that of the choice of lives. The 'moral message' of *Republic* has been to underline the importance of choosing justice over injustice. But when the theme of the choice of lives recurs in the reincarnation section of Er's story, the message is considerably obscured. Instead of the expected account of eternal rewards in heaven for the just person, Er recounts how every soul, whether just or unjust, receives or chooses a new incarnation after its period 'above' or 'below', and how fortunes are often reversed. Some formerly just souls become heedless and make unwise choices for their next life—choices for which, as the priest insists (617e) the chooser, not god, is responsible. Such an outcome—whereby many just souls embark on a new life which will be evil and bad—is surely puzzling. The reader is enchanted by the myth's solemn account of the role of Necessity's daughters, in assigning future life choices, and by its lively description of how familiar characters such as Odysseus and Agamemnon selected their new lives. But the account of reversals of fortune, and of how the soul forgets its past life and its own choosing of the new one, thanks to drinking the draught of neglect in the Plain of Oblivion, makes the promised story of heavenly rewards ambiguous rather than salutary.

L.B.

———

614b 'Well, I'm not going to tell you the kind of saga Alcinous had to endure,'* I said. 'Endurance will be my theme, however—that of brave Er the son of Armenius, who was a Pamphylian by birth. Once upon a time, he was killed in battle, and by the time the corpses were collected, ten days later, they had all putrefied except his, which was still in good shape. He was taken home and, twelve days after his death, just as his funeral was about to start and he was lying on the pyre, he came back to life. Then he told people what he'd seen in the other world.

'He said that his soul left his body and went on a journey, with lots of other souls as his companions. They came to an c awesome place, where they found two openings next to each other in the earth, and two others directly opposite them up in the sky. There were judges* sitting between the openings who made their assessment and then told the moral ones to take the right-hand route which went up and through the sky, and gave them tokens to wear on their fronts to show what behaviour they'd been assessed for, but told the immoral ones to take the left-hand, downward route. These people also had tokens, but on their backs, to show all their past deeds. When Er approached, however, the judges said that he had to report d back to mankind about what goes on there, and they told him to listen and observe everything that happened in the place.

'From where he was, he could see souls leaving, once they'd been judged, by one or other of the two openings in the sky and in the earth, and he noticed how the other two openings were used too: one was for certain souls, caked in grime and dust, to rise out of the earth, while the other was for other, clean souls to come down out of the sky. They arrived e periodically, and he gained the impression that it had taken a long journey for them to get there; they were grateful to turn aside into the meadow* and find a place to settle down. The scene resembled a festival. Old acquaintances greeted one another; those who'd come out of the earth asked those from the heavens what had happened to them there, and were asked the same question in return. The tales of the one group were accompanied by groans and tears, as they recalled all the awful 615a things they'd experienced and seen in the course of their underworld journey (which takes a thousand years),* while the souls from heaven had only wonderful experiences and incredibly beautiful sights to recount.

'It would take ages to tell you a substantial proportion of their tales, Glaucon, but here's a brief outline of what Er said. Each individual had been punished—for every single crime he'd ever committed, and for every person he'd ever wronged—ten times, which is to say once every hundred years b (assuming that the span of human life is a hundred years), to ensure that the penalty he paid was ten times worse than the crime.* Take people who had caused a great many deaths, by betraying a country or an army, and people who had enslaved others or been responsible for inflicting misery in some other way: for every single person they had hurt, they received back ten times the amount of pain. Conversely, the same principle applied to the rewards people received for their good deeds, their morality and justice. Things are different, however, for c those who die at birth or shortly afterwards, but what he told me about them isn't worth mentioning.* However, he did tell a story about the even greater rewards and penalties for obser- vance and non-observance of the proper behaviour towards the gods and one's parents, and for murder with one's own hand.

'He said that he overheard someone asking someone else where Ardiaeus the Great was. (A thousand years earlier, this Ardiaeus had been the dictator of a certain city-state in Pamphylia, and is said to have committed a great many abominable crimes, including killing his aged father and his d elder brother.) The person who'd been asked the question replied, "He's not here, and he never will be. One of the terrible sights we saw was when we were near the exit. At last, after all we'd been through, we were about to come up from underground, when we suddenly caught sight of Ardiaeus. There were others with him, the vast majority of whom had been dictators, while the rest had committed awful non- e political crimes. They were under the impression that they were on the point of leaving, but the exit refused to take them. Whenever anyone whose wickedness couldn't be redeemed tried to go up, or anyone who hadn't been punished enough, it made bellowing sounds. Fierce, fiery-looking men were standing there," he went on, "and they could make sense of the sounds. These men simply grabbed hold of some of the criminals and took them away, but they placed fetters on Ardiaeus' wrists, ankles, and neck, and others got the same 616a treatment; then they threw their prisoners to the ground and flayed them, and finally dragged them away along the roadside, tearing them to pieces on the thorny shrubs. They told any passers-by that they were taking them away to hurl them into Tartarus,* and explained why as well."

'He added that of all the various terrors they experienced there, the worst was the fear they each felt that, as they started their ascent, they'd encounter the bellowing sound, and that there was nothing more gratifying than hearing no sound and making the ascent.

'So much for Er's description of the penalties and punishments, and the equivalent rewards. They spent seven days b in the meadow, and on the eighth day they had to leave and go elsewhere. On the fourth day after that they reached a place from where they could see a straight shaft of light stretching from on high through the heavens and the earth; the light was like a pillar, and it was just like a rainbow in colour, except that it was brighter and clearer. It took another day's travelling to reach the light, and when they got there they were at the mid-point of the light and they could see, stretching away out of the heavens, the extremities of the bonds of the heavens c (for this light binds the heavens together, and as the girth that underpins a trireme holds a trireme together, so this light holds the whole rotation together),* while stretching down from the extremities was the spindle of Necessity, which causes the circular motion of all the separate rotations.

'The spindle's stem and hook are made of adamant, while its whorl consists of various substances, including adamant. In appearance, the whorl basically looks like whorls here on d earth, but, given Er's description, one is bound to picture it as if there were first a large hollow whorl, with its insides completely scooped out, and with a second, smaller one lying snugly inside it (like those jars which fit into one another), and then, on the same arrangement, a third whorl, a fourth

one, and finally four others. For he said that there were eight
e concentric whorls in all, and that their circular rims, looked at
from above, formed a solid surface, as if there were just a single
whorl attached to the stem, which was driven right through
the middle of the eighth whorl.*

'The circle which constituted the rim of the first whorl, the
one on the outside, was the broadest; next broadest was the rim
of the sixth whorl; third was the rim of the fourth whorl;
fourth was the rim of the eighth whorl; fifth was the rim of the
seventh whorl; sixth was the rim of the fifth whorl; seventh
was the rim of the third whorl; and eighth was the rim of the
second whorl.* The rim of the largest whorl was spangled; the
rim of the seventh whorl was brightest; the rim of the eighth
617a whorl gained its colour by reflecting the light of the seventh
one; the rims of the second and fifth whorls were more yellow
than the rest, and were almost identical in hue; the third was
the whitest; the fourth was reddish; the sixth was white, but
not as white as the third.*

'Now, although the rotation of the spindle as a whole was
uniform, nevertheless within the motion of the whole the
seven inner circles moved, at regular speeds, in orbits which
ran counter to the direction of the whole.* The seven inner
circles varied in speed: the eighth was the fastest; then second
b fastest were, all at once, the seventh, sixth, and fifth;* the third
fastest seemed to them (Er said) to be the fourth, which was in
retrograde motion;* the fourth fastest was the third, and
the fifth fastest was the second. The spindle was turning in the
lap of Lady Necessity. Each of the spindle's circles acted as
the vehicle for a Siren. Each Siren, as she stood on one of the
circles, sounded a single note, and all eight notes together
made a single harmonious sound.

c   'Three other women were also sitting on thrones which were
evenly spaced around the spindle. They were the Fates, the
daughters of Necessity, robed in white, with garlands on their
heads; they were Lachesis, Clotho, and Atropos, accompany-
ing the Sirens' song, with Lachesis singing of the past, Clotho

of the present, and Atropos of the future. Clotho periodically laid her right hand on the outer circle of the spindle and helped to turn it; Atropos did the same with her left hand to the inner circles; and Lachesis alternately helped the outer circle and the inner circles on their way with one hand after the other.   d

'As soon as the souls arrived, they had to approach Lachesis. An intermediary arranged them in rows and then, once he'd taken from Lachesis' lap lottery tokens and sample lives, stepped up on to a high rostrum and said, "Hear the words of Lady Lachesis, daughter of Necessity. You souls condemned to impermanence,* the cycle of birth followed by death is beginning again for you. No deity will be assigned to you: you will pick your own deities.* The order of gaining tokens e decides the order of choosing lives, which will be irrevocably yours. Goodness makes its own rules: each of you will be good to the extent that you value it. Responsibility lies with the chooser, not with God."

'After this announcement, he threw the tokens into the crowd, and everybody (except Er, who wasn't allowed to) picked up the token that fell beside him. Each soul's position in the lottery was clear once he'd picked up his token. Next, the intermediary placed on the ground in front of them the 618a sample lives, of which there were far more than there were souls in the crowd; every single kind of human and animal life was included among the samples. For instance, there were dictatorships (some lifelong, others collapsing before their time and ending in poverty, exile, and begging), and also male and female versions of lives of fame for one's physique, good looks, and general strength and athleticism, or for one's b lineage and the excellence of one's ancestors; and there were lives which lacked these distinctions as well. Temperament wasn't included, however, since that inevitably varies according to the life chosen; but otherwise there was every possible combination of qualities with one another and with factors like wealth, poverty, sickness, and health, in extreme or moderate amounts.

'Now, it looks as though this is an absolutely critical point for a person, my dear Glaucon. And that is why every single c one of us has to give his undivided attention—to the detriment of all other areas of study—to trying to track down and discover whether there is anyone he can discover and unearth anywhere who can give him the competence and knowledge to distinguish a good life from a bad one, and to choose the better life from among all the possibilities that surround him at any given moment.* He has to weigh up all the things we've been talking about, so as to know what bearing they have, in combination and in isolation, on living a good life. What are the good or bad results of mixing good looks with d poverty or with wealth, in conjunction with such-and-such a mental condition? What are the effects of the various combinations of innate and acquired characteristics such as high and low birth, involvement and lack of involvement in politics, physical strength and frailty, cleverness and stupidity, and so on? He has to be able to take into consideration the nature of the mind and so make a rational choice, from among all the alternatives, between a better and a worse life. e He has to be in a position to think of a life which leads his mind towards a state of increasing immorality as worse, and consider one which leads in the opposite direction as better. There's no other factor he'll regard as important: we've already seen that this is the cardinal decision anyone has to make, whether he does so during his lifetime or after he's 619a died. By the time he reaches Hades, then, this belief must be absolutely unassailable in him, so that there too he can resist the lure of afflictions such as wealth, and won't be trapped into dictatorship or any other activity which would cause him to commit a number of foul crimes, and to suffer even worse torments himself. Instead, he must know how to choose a life which occupies the middle ground, and how to avoid either extreme, as much as possible, in this world, and throughout the next. For this is how a person guarantees happiness for b himself.

64

'Anyway, according to the report the messenger from the other world delivered on the occasion I'm talking about, the intermediary continued: "Even the last to come forward will find an acceptable life, not a pernicious one, if he chooses wisely and exerts himself during his lifetime. The first to choose should take care, and the last need not despair."

'Er said that no sooner had the intermediary fallen silent than the person whose turn was first stepped up and chose the most powerful dictatorship available. His stupidity and greed* made him choose this life without inspecting it thoroughly and in sufficient detail, so he didn't notice that it included the fate of eating his own children* and committing other horrible c crimes. When he took the time to examine his choice, he beat his breast and wept, but he didn't comply with the intermediary's earlier words, because he didn't hold himself responsible for his afflictions; instead he blamed fortune, the gods, and anything rather than himself. He was one of those who had come out of the heavens, since he'd spent his previous life in a well-regulated community, and so had been good to a certain extent, even though it was habituation rather than philosophy that had made him so. In fact, those who had come d from the heavens fell into this trap more or less as often as the others, since they hadn't learned how to cope with difficult situations, whereas the majority of those who had come out of the earth didn't rush into their decisions, because they knew about suffering from their own experiences as well as from observing others. That was one of the main reasons—another being the unpredictability of the lottery—that most of the souls met with a reversal, from good to bad or vice versa. The point is this: if during his lifetime in this world a person practises philosophy with integrity, and if it so happens, as a result of the lottery, that he's not one of the last to choose, e then the report brought back from that other world makes it plausible to expect not only that he'd be happy here, but also that he'd travel from here to there and back again on the smooth roads of the heavens, rather than on rough underground trails.

'It was well worth seeing, Er said, how particular souls 620a chose their lives; the sight was by turns sad, amusing, and astonishing.* Their choice was invariably dictated by conditioning gained in their former incarnation. For instance, he said he saw the soul which had once belonged to Orpheus choose the life of a swan; because women had killed him, he hated everything female, and wanted to avoid a female incarnation.* He saw Thamyras choose a nightingale's life, while a swan and other songbirds opted for change and chose b to live as human beings. The soul which was twentieth in line picked the life of a lion; it was Ajax the son of Telamon, and he didn't want a human incarnation because he was unable to forget the decision that had been made about the armour.* The next soul was that of Agamemnon: again, his sufferings had embittered him against humanity, and he chose instead to be reborn as an eagle. About halfway through, it was the turn of Atalanta's soul, and she caught sight of a male athlete's life: when she noticed how well rewarded it was, she couldn't walk on by, and she took it. After Atalanta, c Er saw the soul of Epius the son of Panopeus becoming a craftswoman; and later, towards the end, he saw the soul of Thersites the funny man taking on a monkey's form. As the luck of the lottery had it, Odysseus' soul was the very last to come forward and choose. The memory of all the hardship he had previously endured had caused his ambition to subside, so he walked around for a long time, looking for a life as a non-political private citizen. At last he found d one lying somewhere, disregarded by everyone else. When he saw it, he happily took it, saying that he'd have done exactly the same even if he'd been the first to choose. And the same kind of thorough exchange and shuffling of roles occurred in the case of animals too, as they became men or other animals—wild ones if they'd been immoral, tame ones otherwise.

'When the souls had all finished choosing their lives, they approached Lachesis in the order the lottery had assigned them. She gave them all the personal deity they'd selected, to accompany them throughout their lives, as their guardians and to fulfil the choices they had made. Each deity first led its soul e to Clotho, to pass under her hand and under the revolving orbit of the spindle, and so to ratify the destiny the soul had chosen in the lottery. Then, once a connection had been made with her, the deity led the soul to Atropos and her spinning, to make the web woven by Clotho fixed and unalterable.* Afterwards, the soul set a fixed course for Lady Necessity's throne and passed under it; once it was on the other side, 621a and when everyone else had joined it there, they all travelled through terrible, stifling heat (since no trees or plants grew in that place) to the Plain of Oblivion.* Since the day was now drawing to a close, they camped there by the River of Neglect, whose waters no vessel can contain.

'Now, they were all required to drink a certain amount of water, but some were too stupid to look after themselves properly and drank more than the required amount.* As each person drank, he forgot everything. They lay down to b sleep, and in the middle of the night there was thunder and an earthquake. All of a sudden, they were lifted up from where they were, and they darted like shooting stars* away in various directions for rebirth. As for Er, although he hadn't been allowed to drink any of the water, he had no idea what direction he took, or how he got back to his body, but he suddenly opened his eyes and found that it was early in the morning and that he was lying on the funeral pyre.*

'There you are then, Glaucon. The story has made it safely through to the end,* without perishing on the way. And it might save us too, if we take it to heart, and so successfully c cross the River of Oblivion without defiling our souls. Anyway, my recommendation would be for us to regard the soul as immortal and as capable of surviving a great deal of suffering, just as it survives all the good times. We should always keep to the upward path, and we should use every means at our disposal to act morally and with intelligence, so that we may gain our own and the gods' approval, not only during our stay here on earth, but also when we collect the prizes our morality has earned us, which will be just as extensive as the rewards victorious athletes receive from all quarters. And then, both here and during the thousand-year journey of our story,* all will be well with us.'

8. THE WINGED SOUL
(*Phaedrus* 246a–257a)

Plato's consummate literary skills are seen at their best in the dialogue *Phaedrus*. The very opening of the work, with its enticing description of Socrates' walk *à deux* with the younger Phaedrus alongside the River Ilissus, draws the reader into an unusually intimate conversation. Phaedrus, fresh from attending a display by the orator Lysias, is keen to rehearse for Socrates the orator's ingenious but perverse speech about love. Its theme was advice to a beautiful boy: yield your favours not to an older man who loves you, but to one who does not. Next Socrates caps Lysias' speech with a finer one of his own on the same theme, but soon repents and seeks to make amends for competing with Lysias on his own terms. Both had spoken shamelessly about Love, and had dwelt on the jealousy and quarrels of lovers.

Now Socrates will speak a second time about Love; like the poet Stesichorus, he will offer a recantation, taking back his earlier libels. The myth of the winged soul and the poetic discourse on Love which form this extract are the heart of the speech, but first there are other revelations for Phaedrus. Madness, condemned in Socrates' earlier speech, is now praised; it takes many forms, of which that of the lover is one. 'Madness is given by the gods, to allow us to achieve the greatest good fortune.' Next comes a proof that the soul is immortal—and here divine and human souls are not distinguished; the ground for the proof is the soul's essence as a self-moving thing. The thesis of the immortality of the soul is familiar from *Phaedo* (see 'The Other World'), but this proof is a novelty.

To reveal more of the nature of the soul, Socrates turns to the image which opens this extract. The souls of gods and men are composite; they are compared to a charioteer with a team of horses. In gods all soul-parts are good, but in human souls the charioteer drives two disparate horses, one good, one bad. Before incarnation as a human, a soul travels in the heavens, like a winged team with its charioteer, in company with the gods, gazing on true reality.

Depending on the conduct of its horses, the soul will see much, little, or none of these wonders (248a–b). Next, weighed down to earth and clad in human flesh, souls enter a variety of life-types; they forget what they beheld in the heavens. But the sight of a beautiful boy will recall, for the lover, beauty itself; the powerful emotions aroused by falling in love with such a boy may cause the soul's wings to grow again, but a conflict between the soul's horses (that is, between its good and its base impulses) will ensue. In an intensely sensual description of love and sexual desire, Socrates depicts the struggles between physical desire and the higher feelings for the beloved, struggles which, in the philosophical soul, will culminate in a self-mastery which brings the most elevated mutual love, blessedness, and harmony.

Towards the end of his speech, Socrates describes, first, the truly philosophical lovers who master their passions (256a–b). Then, seemingly with equal tenderness, he depicts pairs of lovers who briefly yield to their desires, then remain attached throughout their lives (256c–d); they too can hope for wings in the life to come, thanks to their love. Whereas the description of Love in Diotima's speech (see 'The Birth of Love') seemed to deprive it of the special concern of a lover for a particular person, here we find a description of a love (always between men) which is less self-centred, which cares more for the soul of the beloved, and which is a love, not of the Beautiful itself, but of its manifestation in another human being.

L.B.

———

246a 'That is enough about the soul's immortality. I must now say something about its character. It would take too long—and beyond the slightest shadow of a doubt require a god—to explain its character, but the use of an analogy will make the task within lesser human powers. So let's do that. In my analogy, a soul is like an organic whole made up of a charioteer and his team of horses.* Now, while the horses and charioteers of gods are always thoroughly good, those of everyone else are
b a mixture.* Although our inner ruler drives a pair of horses,

only one of his horses is thoroughly noble and good, while the other is thoroughly the opposite. This inevitably makes driving, in our case, difficult and disagreeable.

'Next I must try to explain how one living creature is called "immortal" while another is called "mortal".* It is the job of the soul in general to look after all that is inanimate,* and souls patrol the whole universe, taking on different forms at different times. A complete soul—which is to say, one that is winged—journeys on high and controls the whole world, but c one that has lost its wings is carried along until it seizes upon something solid, and it takes up residence there. The earthly body of which it takes control seems to move itself, but that is the effect of the soul, and the whole unit of soul and body conjoined is called a "living creature", and also "mortal". No one who has thought the matter through could call a living creature "immortal", but because we have never seen a god, and have an inadequate conception of godhood, we imagine a kind of immortal living creature, possessing both soul and d body in an everlasting combination. Anyway, we can leave the facts of this matter to be and be expressed however the gods like, but we have to come to some understanding of what causes a soul to shed and lose its wings. It is something like this.

'The natural property of a wing is to carry something heavy aloft, up on high to the abode of the gods. There is a sense in which, of all the things that are related to the body, wings have more of the divine in them. Anything divine is good, wise, virtuous, and so on, and so these qualities are the best source e of nourishment and growth for the soul's wings, but badness and evil and so on cause them to shrink and perish.

'The supreme leader in the heavens is Zeus. He goes at the head, in a winged chariot, arranging and managing everything, and behind him comes the host of gods and spirits, in an orderly array of eleven squadrons.* For Hestia stays alone in 247a the gods' house, while each of the other gods who have been assigned one of the twelve positions takes his place at the head of the rank to which he has been assigned. So there are many glorious sights to be seen within heaven, and many wonderful paths along which the favoured company of gods go and return, each performing his proper function,* and the gods are accompanied by everyone who wants to join them and is capable of doing so, because meanness has no place in the gods' choir. When they turn to food and go to one of their banquets,

b they journey skyward to the rim of the heavenly vault. Although the way is steep, the gods' chariots make light of the journey, since they are well balanced and easy to handle, but the other chariots find it hard, because the troublesome horse weighs them down. Any charioteer who has trained this horse imperfectly finds that it pulls him down towards the earth and holds him back, and this is the point at which a soul faces the worst suffering and the hardest struggle.

'When the souls we call "immortal"* reach the rim, they make their way to the outside and stand on the outer edge of

c heaven, and as they stand there the revolution carries them around, while they gaze outward from the heaven. The region beyond heaven has never yet been adequately described in any of our earthly poets' compositions, nor will it ever be. But since one has to make a courageous attempt to speak the truth, especially when it is truth that one is speaking about, here is a description. This region is filled with true being. True being has no colour or form; it is intangible, and visible only to intelligence, the soul's guide. True being is the province of

d everything that counts as true knowledge. So since the mind of god is nourished by intelligence and pure knowledge (as is the mind of every soul which is concerned to receive its proper food), it is pleased to be at last in a position to see true being, and in gazing on the truth it is fed and feels comfortable, until the revolution carries it around to the same place again. In the course of its circuit it observes justice as it really is, self-control, knowledge—not the kind of knowledge that is involved with change and differs according to which of the

e various existing things (to use the term "existence" in its everyday sense) it makes its object, but the kind of knowledge whose object is things as they really are. And once it has feasted its gaze in the same way on everything else that really is, it sinks back into the inside of heaven and returns home.* Once back home, the soul's charioteer reins in his horses by their manger, throws them ambrosia to eat, and gives them nectar to wash the ambrosia down.*

'This is how the gods live. As for the other souls, any that 248a have closely followed a god and have come to resemble him most* raise the heads of their charioteers into the region outside and are carried around along with the revolution, but they are disturbed by their horses and their view of things as they really are is uncertain. Others poke their heads through from time to time, but sink back down in between, and so they see some things, but miss others, depending on the resistance offered by their horses. The rest all long for the upper region and follow after, but they cannot break through, and they are carried around under the surface, trampling and bumping into one another as one tries to overtake another. So there is b utter chaos, nothing but sweat and conflict. In the course of this confusion many souls are crippled as a result of the incompetence of the charioteers, and many have their wings severely damaged, but even after all this effort none of them succeeds in seeing things as they really are before having to return and rely on specious nourishment.*

'The reason why there is so much determination to see the whereabouts of the plain of truth* is not only that the proper food for the best part of the soul happens to come from the meadow there, but also that it is in the nature of the wings c which raise the soul to be nourished by this region. It is the decree of destiny that any soul which attends a god and catches even a glimpse of the truth remains free from injury until the next revolution, and if it is able to do this every time, it will continue to be free from harm. But souls which fall behind and lose their vision of the truth, and are for some unfortunate reason or another weighed down by being filled with forgetfulness and weakness, lose their wings thanks to this burden and fall to earth. At this point they are subject to a

d law that they are not to be planted into the bodies of animals in their first incarnation. The souls which have seen the most are to enter the seeds of men who will become philosophers, lovers of beauty, men of culture, men who are dedicated to love;* the second group those of law-abiding kings or military commanders or civic leaders; the third group those of politicians, estate-managers or businessmen; the fourth group those of men who love exercising in a gymnasium or future experts in bodily health; the fifth group will live as prophets or as initiators into one of the mystery cults,* the sixth group will

e most suitably live as poets or some other kind of representative artist, the seventh as artisans or farmers, the eighth as sophists or demagogues, and the ninth as tyrants.*

'In all these cases anyone who has lived a moral life will obtain a better fate, and anyone who has lived an immoral life the opposite.* For no soul returns to the place it fell from for ten thousand years*—it takes that long for wings to grow

249a again—except the soul of a man who has practised philosophy with sincerity or combined his love for a boy with the practice of philosophy. At the completion of the third thousand-year circuit, if these souls have chosen the philosophical life three times in succession, they regain their wings and in the three-thousandth year they return.* But all the other souls are judged after the end of their first life, and once they have been judged they either go to prisons in the underworld where they are punished, or are raised aloft by Justice to a certain place in the heavens and live as they deserve, depending on how they

b lived when they were in human form.* But in the thousandth year both groups of souls come for the allotment and choice of their second life and each of them chooses the life it likes.* This is the point at which a human soul can be reincarnated as an animal, and someone who was formerly human can be reborn as a human being once again, instead of being an animal. For a soul which has never seen the truth cannot enter into human form, because a man must understand the impressions he receives by reference to classes: he draws on the plurality of perceptions to combine them by reasoning into a c single class. This is recollection of the things which our souls once saw during their journey as companions to a god, when they saw beyond the things we now say "exist" and poked their heads up into true reality.* That is why only the mind of a philosopher deserves to grow wings, because it uses memory to remain always as close as possible to those things proximity to which gives a god his divine qualities. By making correct use of reminders of these things a man, being constantly initiated into the most perfect rites of all, becomes the only one who is truly perfect. But since he is remote from human concerns and close to divinity, he is criticized by the general run of mankind d as deranged, because they do not realize that he is possessed by a god.

'Now we reach the point to which the whole discussion of the fourth kind of madness was tending. This fourth kind of madness is the kind which occurs when someone sees beauty here on earth and is reminded of true beauty. His wings begin to grow and he wants to take to the air on his new plumage, but he cannot; like a bird he looks upwards, and because he ignores what is down here, he is accused of behaving like a madman.* So the point is that this turns out to be the most thoroughly e good of all kinds of possession, not only for the man who is possessed, but also for anyone who is touched by it,* and the word "lover" refers to a lover of beauty who has been possessed by this kind of madness.* For, as I have already said, the soul of every human being is bound to have seen things as they really are, or else it would not have entered this kind of living creature.

'But not every soul is readily prompted by things here on 250a earth to recall those things that are real. This is not easy for souls which caught only a brief glimpse of things there, nor for those which after falling to earth have suffered the misfortune of being perverted and made immoral by the company they keep and have forgotten the sacred things they saw then. When the remaining few, whose memories are good enough, see a likeness here which reminds them of things there, they are amazed and beside themselves, but they do not understand what is happening to them because of a certain unclarity in their perceptions. But although the likenesses here on earth

b (of things which are precious to souls, such as justice and self-control) lack all lustre, and only a few people come to them and barely see, through dim sense organs, what it is that any likeness is a likeness of, yet earlier it was possible for them to see beauty in all its brilliance. That was when—we as attendants of Zeus* and others of one of the other gods—as part of a happy company they saw a wonderful sight and spectacle and were initiated into what we may rightly call the most wonder-

c ful of the mysteries. When we celebrated these mysteries then, we were not only perfect beings ourselves, untouched by all the troubles which awaited us later, but we also were initiated into and contemplated things shown to us that were perfect, simple, stable, and blissful. We were surrounded by rays of pure light, being pure ourselves and untainted by this object we call a "body" and which we carry around with us now, imprisoned like shellfish.*

'Let this be my tribute to memory; it was remembering and longing for those past events which has made me go on rather too long now.* But turning to beauty, it shone out, as I said,

d among its companions there, and once here on earth we found, by means of the clearest of our senses, that it sparkles with particular clarity. For the keenest kind of perception the body affords us is the one that comes through seeing, though we are not able to see wisdom because, as with everything else which is an object of love, wisdom would cause terrible pangs of love in us if it presented some kind of clear image of itself by approaching our organ of sight. But as things are, it is only beauty which has the property of being especially visible and

e especially lovable.* Anyone who was initiated long ago or who has been corrupted is not given to moving rapidly from here to there, towards beauty as it really is. Instead, he gazes on its namesake here on earth, and the upshot is that the sight does not arouse reverence in him. No, he surrenders to pleasure and tries like an animal to mount his partner and to father offspring, and having become habituated to excess he is not afraid or ashamed to pursue unnatural pleasures.* But when someone who has only recently been initiated, and who took in plenty of the sights to be seen then, sees a marvellous face or a bodily form which is a good reflection of beauty, at first he shivers and is gripped by something like the fear he felt then, and the sight also moves him to revere his beloved as if he were a god. In fact, it is only concern about being thought completely insane that stops him from sacrificing to his beloved as if he were a cult statue or a god.*

251a

'Following this sight, the kind of change comes over him that you would expect after a shivering fit, and he begins to sweat and to run an unusually high fever, because the reception through his eyes of the effusion of beauty causes him to get hot. Now, this effusion is also the natural means of irrigating his wings. His heat softens the coat covering the feathers' buds, which had been too hard and closed up for wings to grow. As further nourishment pours in, the quills of the feathers swell and begin to grow from the roots upwards and to spread all over the underside of the soul, because previously the whole soul was winged. At this point, then, his whole soul seethes and pounds—in fact, the soul of someone who is beginning to grow wings experiences exactly the same sensations as children feel when they are teething, with their teeth just starting to grow, and they feel an itching and a soreness in their gums. So the soul, as it grows its wings, seethes and feels sore and tingles.

b

c

'When it gazes on the young man's beauty, and receives the particles emanating from it as they approach and flow in— which, of course, is why we call it desire*—it is watered and heated, and it recovers from its pain and is glad. But when it is away from the boy and becomes parched, the dryness makes

d

77

the mouths of the channels for the budding feathers close up and contain the wings' new growth. The new shoots are shut up inside along with the desire. They throb like pulsing veins, and each one rubs against its channel, with the result that the whole soul stings all over and is frantic with pain—until it remembers the boy in his beauty and is glad. The strange sensation of mingled pain and pleasure is agony for it, and its
e helplessness torments it. It is too disturbed to sleep at night or stay still by day, and it rushes around to wherever it thinks it might see the boy who bears the beauty it longs for. The sight of him opens the irrigation channels of desire and frees the former blockage; it finds relief and an end to the stinging pain, and once more enjoys this, for the time being, as the
252a most intense pleasure. This is not something it willingly does without, and it values no one more than the beautiful boy. It is oblivious to mothers, brothers, and all its friends. It does not care in the slightest if its wealth suffers through neglect. It despises all the customs and good manners on which it had previously prided itself. Indeed, it is ready to play the part of a slave and to sleep wherever it is allowed to, as long as it is as close as possible to the object of its desire. For as well as worshipping the boy who bears the beauty, it has discovered that
b he is also the only one who can cure it of its terrible suffering.

'This, you beautiful boy, to whom I am addressing this speech—this is the experience men call love, but you are probably too young to think of what the gods call it as anything but a joke. I think that some Homeric scholars recite two verses from the unpublished poems of Homer which have to do with Love. The second of the two verses is quite outrageous and not very metrical at all. The couplet goes like this:

> He is the winged one that mortals call "Eros",
> But since he must grow wings the gods call him "Pteros".*

c You can believe this or not, as you wish. But at any rate the background to and experience of being in love are as I have said.

'Now, if the captive is one of the attendants of Zeus, he can endure the burden of the Winged One with some dignity. But things are different when the servants of Ares, who made the circuitous journey in his company, are captured by Love. If they have the slightest inkling that they have been wronged by their beloved, they become murderous: they are quite ready to immolate both themselves and their beloveds. And so it goes for every single god: as long as he has not yet been corrupted and is living the first of his lives here on earth, an individual spends his life honouring and imitating to the best of his ability the god to whose chorus he belongs, and in all his d dealings and relations, including his love-affairs, he conforms to this mode of behaviour. So which good-looking boy an individual chooses as his beloved depends on his disposition, and he treats the boy as if he were that very god: he constructs for himself an image, so to speak, and decorates it in order to worship his god and celebrate his rites.

'The followers of Zeus, then, want someone with a Zeus- e like soul as their beloved. They look for someone with the potential to be a philosopher and a leader, and when they find him and have fallen in love with him, they do all they can to develop this potential in him. If they have not undertaken such a task before, they set about it now, by learning from any available sources and searching by themselves. In hunting on 253a their own for the nature of their god, they are helped by the intense compulsion they are under of gazing on the god.* Since they are in contact with the god in their memories, they are inspired by him and, in so far as it is possible for a mortal man to partake of a god, they derive their way of life and the things they do from him. And because they hold their beloved responsible for this, they feel even more affection for him, and as if Zeus were a well from which they draw water, Bacchant-like* they pour it over their beloved's soul and make him as similar to their own god as they can.

'Those who were in Hera's company, on the other hand, b look for a boy with kingly qualities, and when they find him

they behave in exactly the same way with him. And the followers of Apollo and each of the other gods proceed in the same
way, in accordance with the nature of their god, and look for a
boy for themselves who has the same qualities as themselves.*
When they find him, they not only imitate the god themselves,
but also, by means of persuasion and attunement, they get the
boy to conform, as much as he can, to the god's way of life and
characteristics. There is no malice or mean-spirited ill-will in
their dealings with their beloveds.* No, they behave as they do
because they are trying their utmost to get the boy completely
c and utterly to resemble themselves and the god to whom they
are dedicated. What true lovers are committed to, the con-
summation of their quest—at any rate, if they attain their goal
in the way I have been describing—thus becomes admirable
and a way for someone who is maddened by love to secure the
happiness of the object of his affection, if he captures him.

'I will now describe how a captive is caught. Let's stick to
the threefold division of the soul we made at the start of
this tale, with each and every soul consisting of two horse-like
d aspects and a third like a charioteer. Now, we said that one of
the horses was good and the other bad, but we did not describe
the goodness of the good one and the badness of the bad one.
We must do so now. The one in the better position* has an
upright appearance, and is clean-limbed, high-necked, hook-
nosed, white in colour, and dark-eyed; his determination to
succeed is tempered by self-control and respect for others,
which is to say that he is an ally of true glory; and he needs no
whip, but is guided only by spoken commands.* The other is
e crooked, over-large, a haphazard jumble of limbs; he has a
thick, short neck, and a flat face; he is black in colour, with
grey, bloodshot eyes, an ally of excess and affectation, hairy
around the ears, hard of hearing, and scarcely to be controlled
with a combination of whip and goad.

'So when the charioteer sees the light of his beloved's eyes,
his whole soul is suffused with a sensation of heat and he is
254a filled with the tingling and pricking of desire. The horse that

is obedient to the charioteer restrains itself from leaping on its beloved, because as always it is held back by a sense of shame. The other horse, however, stops paying any attention to the charioteer's goad and whip; it prances and lunges forward violently, making life extremely difficult for its team-mate and for the charioteer, and compelling them to head towards the beloved and bring up the subject of the pleasures of sex.* At first, these two get annoyed at being forced to behave in a way that seems dreadfully wrong, and put up some resistance, b but eventually, finding no end to their troubles, they let themselves be led forward, and they passively submit to doing as they are told. And so they come close to their beloved and see the lightning-bright beauty of his face. At this sight the charioteer's memory is taken back to the nature of true beauty, and he sees it again in place on a holy pedestal, next to self-control.* The vision terrifies him and he rears back in awe— which inevitably makes him pull back on the reins as well with enough force to set both horses down on their haunches, the c one willingly because of its obedience and the unruly one with a great deal of reluctance.

'After the two horses have withdrawn some way back, the good one drenches the whole soul in sweat brought on by its shame and horror, while the other, once it has got over the pain caused by the bit and its fall, scarcely takes time to draw breath before bursting out into furious abuse and hurling curses at both the charioteer and its team-mate for being cowardly and gutless deserters and defaulters. Once more it tries to force them to approach, against their wills, but it reluctantly agrees d to their request to wait until later. When the proposed time arrives, it reminds them of their promise, while they both feign forgetfulness, and so, plunging and neighing, it forcibly drags them up to the beloved again in order to make the same suggestion to him as before. As they get close, with head lowered and tail out straight, it bites down on the bit and shamelessly drags them on. But then the same thing happens again to the charioteer, only even more strongly: he recoils as if from e a trap and even more violently wrenches the unruly horse's bit back out of its teeth, splashing its curse-laden tongue and jaws with blood, pinning its legs and haunches to the ground, and causing it pain. Once the same thing has happened to it over and over again, the bad horse calms down, and now that it has been humbled it lets itself be guided by the charioteer's intentions. Now, when it sees the good-looking boy, it is frightened to death, and the upshot is that at last the lover's soul follows his beloved in reverence and awe.*

255a 'Not only is the boy now being treated as godlike and receiving every kind of service from a man who is not merely pretending to be in love, but does genuinely feel it, but also it is natural for him to feel affection for someone who is treating him so well. As a result, even if previously he had been put off by the assertion of his school friends or whoever that associating with a lover was wrong, and had therefore repelled his lover's advances, yet now, with the passage of time, increasing maturity induces him to allow him into his com-

b pany, and he is compelled to do so also by necessity, in the sense that it is fated that bad men can never be friends and that good men can never fail to be friends. Once he has allowed him in and has accepted his conversation and company, experience from close at hand of the lover's good will astonishes the beloved and he realizes that the friendship of all his other friends and relatives put together does not amount to even a fraction of the friendship offered by a lover who is inspired by a god.

'When the lover has been doing this for some time, and there has been physical contact between them at meetings

c in the gymnasium and elsewhere, then at last the flowing stream (which Zeus called "desire" when he was in love with Ganymede*) pours down on the lover in such great quantities that while some of it sinks into him, the rest flows off outside as he fills up and brims over. Just as a gust of wind or an echo rebounds from smooth, hard objects and returns to where it came from, so the flow of beauty returns into the beautiful boy through his eyes, which is its natural route into the soul, and when it arrives and excites him, it irrigates his wings' channels d and makes his plumage start to grow, and fills the soul of the beloved in his turn with love. So he is in love, but he has no idea what he is in love with. He does not know what has happened to him and he cannot explain it. It is as if he has caught an inflammation of the eye from someone else and cannot say where it came from;* he fails to appreciate that he is seeing himself in his lover as in a mirror. When his lover is with him, he finds just as much relief from his pain as the lover does; when his lover is not there, he misses him just as much and is missed just as much. He has contracted counter-love as a reflection of his lover's love, but he calls it and thinks of e it as friendship rather than love. His desires are more or less the same as his lover's, though weaker—to see, touch, kiss, lie down together—and as you might expect before long this is exactly what he does.

'When they lie together, the lover's undisciplined horse makes suggestions to the charioteer and demands a little pleasure to reward it for all its pains. The boy's undisciplined 256a horse has nothing to say, but in its desire and confusion embraces the lover and kisses him. It welcomes him as some-one who clearly has its best interests at heart, and when they are lying down together it is inclined not to refuse to play its part in gratifying any request the lover might make. Its team-mate, however, sides with the charioteer and resists this inclination by arguments designed to appeal to its sense of shame. If the better aspects of their minds win and steer them towards orderly conduct and philosophy, they live a wonder-ful, harmonious life here on earth, a life of self-control and b restraint, since they have enslaved the part which allowed evil into the soul and freed the part which allowed goodness in. And when they die, as winged and soaring beings they have won the first of the three truly Olympic bouts,* which brings greater benefits than either human sanity or divine madness can supply.

'But if they live a more ordinary life, devoted to prestige
c rather than philosophy,* it is certainly possible, I imagine,
that when they are drunk or otherwise in a careless state
the two undisciplined horses in them might find their souls
undefended and bring them together, and so that they might
choose the course which is considered the most wonderful of
all by the common run of mankind, and consummate their
relationship. Having once done so, they continue with this
course of action in the future, but not often, because what they
did was not approved by their whole minds. This pair too
spend their lives as friends (though not as close friends as the
others), not only while they are in love, but also when they
d have left love behind. They think they have exchanged vows
of such enormous strength that it would be wrong for them
ever to break them and fall out with each other. At the end
of their lives, when they leave their bodies, they may not have
any wings, but they do have the desire to gain them, and this
is no small prize to have gained from the madness of love.
For it is a law that those who have already made a start on the
skyward journey shall no longer go into the darkness and
enter upon the journey downward to the underworld. Instead,
they live a life of brightness and happily travel in each other's
e company, and sooner or later, thanks to their love, gain their
wings together.

'All these are the divine gifts you will gain from the friendship of a lover, young man. But since the companionship of a
non-lover is tempered by human sanity, it delivers meagre and
mortal rewards. It breeds in the soul of one of its friends a
quality of slavishness which is commonly praised as virtue,
257a and so makes it circle mindlessly around and under the earth
for nine thousand years.*

9. THE TWO COSMIC ERAS

(*Statesman* 268d–274e)

The conversation in Plato's *Statesman* is conducted between the chief speaker, a nameless philosopher visiting Athens (called simply the Stranger from Elea), and a young man confusingly called Socrates (Socrates too takes part in this conversation; but we can easily distinguish his contribution from that of the young Socrates). Much of the Stranger's discourse employs and illustrates the so-called 'method of division', with the aim of arriving at a definition of the statesman, or king.

After several pages of somewhat dry attempts at definition, the Stranger notes that they have so far identified the statesman as the herdsman and rearer of the human herd (that is, of the herd of human beings)—a sort of shepherd. But so far he has not been properly distinguished from impostors, from false claimants to the title. To get clearer on the question, says the Stranger, we shall introduce some light relief in the form of 'part of a great myth'. Ostensibly, then, the myth's function is to advance the search for a correct understanding of the statesman—hence its unusual place early on in the work, not at the very close as so often in the dialogues.

While the story can be seen as some kind of response by Plato to Protagoras' myth about the origin of society and civic virtue (see 'The Origin of Virtue'), the *Statesman*'s myth is more ambitious, more elaborate and far more puzzling. It presents itself as a rationalization of several earlier myths: that of the quarrel between Atreus and Thyestes, of the sun's brief reversal of its course, and stories of earth-born human beings. The resulting account is a fantastical story, told in a deliberately elliptical and confusing manner, about different cosmic eras, separated by a violent reversal of direction of the cosmos.

The myth tells of a period under the rule of Cronus—the Golden Age when there was need for neither human toil nor politics; of cosmic turning which results in the old becoming young, the white-haired returning to black and thence to babyhood;

of a divine helmsman regaining the tiller and setting the cosmos to rights; and much else. Readers will enjoy the challenge of disentangling, ordering, and numbering the myth's elements. They may discern (as do most readings) just two cosmic eras, that of Cronus and the present one, ruled by Zeus; or they may favour a rival reading of three such eras, adding one in between when no deity is in charge. They may simply relish the cosmological fantasies and the humorous elements, such as the question: did the earliest humans of the age of Cronus, who could converse with animals, spend their time discussing philosophy, or merely swapping good stories (272b)? Plato can surely not have intended this myth to contain serious cosmology; his *Timaeus*, with its solemn and extended 'likely story' comes the closest to supplying that.

What morals are to be drawn, if any, about the nature of the true statesman, or the true king? One is clear: to call him a herdsman and rearer of human herds was to confuse the role of the shepherd of the Golden Age with the role of a human statesman today. Today's statesman is a man, not a god, who must rule over those of the same kind as himself, so he is no kind of shepherd. And today's state is one where human toil and human politics are required. One feature remains prominent as the dialogue progresses: the statesman's claim to his title rests on the nature of his expertise. It is a human expertise, but one which weaves together all the elements of a state, including all the subordinate but necessary skills in a state such as that of the judge and the general; in so doing statesmanship controls and is superior to them all.

L.B.

268d STRANGER: We had better take another starting-point, then, and travel by a different road.

YOUNG SOCRATES: What road shall we take?

STRANGER: We should blend in a bit of light relief, as it were, and help ourselves to a lengthy fragment of a great myth, before returning for the rest of the discussion to the
e   previous method of separating one part from another and

gaining the summit we're after that way. Do you think this is what we should do?

YOUNG SOCRATES: Yes.

STRANGER: So pay very careful attention to the myth, then, as if you were a child listening to a story. In any case, you haven't left childhood far behind yet.

YOUNG SOCRATES: Please go on.

STRANGER: Among the ancient tales which have often been repeated and will continue to be told in the future too, the particular event I'm thinking of is the miracle which happened at the time of Atreus' and Thyestes' famous quarrel. I'm sure you're familiar with the story and remember what's supposed to have happened.*

YOUNG SOCRATES: I suppose you mean the portent of the golden lamb.

STRANGER: No, I mean the change that took place in the 269a rising and setting of the sun and the other heavenly bodies. It's said that in those days they used to set where they rise nowadays, and rise on the opposite side of the earth, and that the god* changed things over to the present system then, as an act of testimony for Atreus.

YOUNG SOCRATES: Yes, that's part of the story too.

STRANGER: There are also a lot of stories about Cronus' rule and kingdom.

YOUNG SOCRATES: Yes, very many indeed. b

STRANGER: And it's also said that in the old days people used to be born from the earth, rather than from other human beings.

YOUNG SOCRATES: Yes, that's another of the things we're told used to happen in ancient times.

STRANGER: Well, every one of these things is the result of a single incident. In fact, they are the least remarkable of all the countless consequences of this incident, but because it all happened such a long time ago, the other events have either been forgotten or have become scattered, with their various parts now forming separate stories. None of the

stories tells us of the incident which caused all these events,
c   however, but I had better do so, because it will help us in our
attempt to understand kingship.

YOUNG SOCRATES: That's a very good idea. Do please tell us
the story, and don't leave anything out.

STRANGER: All right. Periodically, this universe of ours is
under the guidance of the god himself, and at these times he
helps it on its circling way, but there are also times—when it
has spun around for the appropriate amount of time—when
he releases it. It then revolves back again in the opposite
direction under its own impulse, since it is a living creature
d   and has been granted intelligence by its original constructor.
There is a particular reason why this ability to retrace its
path is bound to be an inherent part of its make-up.

YOUNG SOCRATES: And what is that?

STRANGER: Only the most divine entities have the property
of remaining for ever in an unchanging, self-identical
state, and any material thing is not of this order. However,
although the creator of what we call heaven or the cosmos
granted it a great many enviable qualities, it is at least par-
e   tially material,* and therefore it cannot be completely free
from change. Nevertheless, in so far as it is within its power
to do so, it keeps to the same place and restricts the change
it undergoes to a single, stable form of motion. So the
reason it has the ability to revolve in the opposite direction
is that this reversal is the smallest possible deviation from
its former motion. There is nothing which is always the
source of its own motion, except perhaps the initiator of all
motion,* and it would be blasphemous to suggest that *this*
moves at different times in opposite directions.

All this rules out three ideas: first, that the cosmos is
always the source of its own motion; second, that it is always
the god who is turning the cosmos as a whole, in both of its
270a   conflicting directions; third, that its movements are due to a
pair of gods with conflicting purposes.* The only position
we're left with, then, is the one we've just expressed: that

the universe is sometimes helped on its way by a divine cause external to itself (and during this period its maker* renews its life and replenishes its store of immortality), while at other times it is released and moves under its own impulse. And it is let go at the critical moment, to enable it to retrace its path for hundreds of thousands of cycles, thanks to its enormous mass, its perfect balance, and the tiny 'foot' it uses for travelling.*

YOUNG SOCRATES: Your whole account sounds very plausible b to me.

STRANGER: Then let's use it as a basis for rational thinking and see if we can come to some understanding of the incident which, I suggested, caused all those remarkable things to happen. I'll tell you exactly what the incident was.

YOUNG SOCRATES: What?

STRANGER: It's the fact that the universe sometimes revolves in the direction it is currently taking, but sometimes goes in the opposite direction.

YOUNG SOCRATES: What do you mean?

STRANGER: Of all the reversals that take place in the heavens, we are bound to think that there is none greater or more c thorough than this.

YOUNG SOCRATES: That seems likely.

STRANGER: So we are also bound to think that this is the time when we inhabitants of the universe experience the greatest changes.

YOUNG SOCRATES: That seems likely too.

STRANGER: But isn't it obvious that it is hard for living creatures to endure many violent and various changes at once?

YOUNG SOCRATES: Of course.

STRANGER: So this must be a time when creatures in general suffer widespread destruction, and when the human race in particular is all but wiped out. A lot of remarkable d and extraordinary things happen to the survivors, but one, which is a consequence of the unwinding of the universe that occurs when the reversal of its present direction occurs, is particularly important.

YOUNG SOCRATES: What is that?

STRANGER: At first, every living creature stayed just as old as it was and every mortal thing stopped getting older in appearance; then they all went into reverse and started

e   growing younger, as it were, and more tender. Old people's white hair grew dark; bearded men's cheeks became smooth and regained the lost bloom of youth; as the days and nights passed, young people's bodies became smoother and smaller and they reverted to a state which was no different, mentally as well as physically, from infancy; then their bodies, which were by now fading fast, just completely disappeared. And the corpses of people who met with violent deaths during this period went through exactly the same changes in a short

271a space of time, so that within a few days their bodies had deteriorated and vanished.

YOUNG SOCRATES: But, sir, how were creatures born in those days? How did parents produce offspring?

STRANGER: Quite simply, Socrates, they didn't: there was no such thing at that time as parental procreation. It was the earth-born race, whose existence once upon a time we hear of in our stories, which was born: that was the time when they began to rise up again out of the earth. Our earliest ancestors, who were the immediate neighbours in time of

b   the end of that former cycle, though they were born at the beginning of the present cycle, left records of the existence of the earth-born race. They passed these stories on to us— stories which nowadays are commonly disbelieved, though they don't deserve to be. You have to look at the matter from a particular point of view and then you can understand it, I think. I mean, it's in keeping with the idea of old people turning into children that people would re-form in the earth where they were lying after their deaths and would come back to life from there, in conformity with the reversal undergone by all natural cycles. Any people who were not gathered up by the god for some other destiny,* therefore, necessarily formed an earth-born race in this way. That is c why they are called 'earth-born', and that is the origin of the legend.

YOUNG SOCRATES: Yes, this is perfectly consistent with the earlier parts of your account. But you also mentioned life under Cronus' regime.* Did this happen when the heavenly bodies had reversed the direction they took before, or the direction they take now? I mean, it goes without saying that a change in the motion of the sun and the heavenly bodies takes place during both reversals.

STRANGER: You've followed the discussion well. As for your question, there isn't the slightest trace in the current cycle d of things just happening without people having to put in any effort; this is another feature of the former cycle. For that was when the god first began to rule and to take charge of the actual rotation as a whole, and the same thing happened domain by domain as well, with the parts of the cosmos being exhaustively divided between various tutelary gods. To take living creatures in particular, a different divine spirit was assigned to each species and each flock, to act as its herdsman, so to speak. Each spirit had sole responsibility for supplying all the needs of the creatures in his charge. As a result, there was no savage behaviour, such e as creatures preying on one another, and fights and disputes were completely unknown.

Thousands of examples could be given of other consequences of this arrangement, but I'll tell you the reasons for the stories about people living an effortless life. A god was directly responsible for managing the human herd, just as nowadays, because they are closer to godhood, humans herd inferior species. With the god as their herdsman, there was no organized society, no marriage, and no children, because everyone just came back to life out of the earth, with no 272a memory of the past. But although they didn't have anything like this, trees and other plants produced huge crops and

grew in abundance, without needing to be farmed: the soil yielded them of its own accord. People spent most of their time roaming around in the open air without clothes or bedding, since the climate was temperate and caused them no distress, and the earth produced more than enough grass
b for them to lie on in comfort. That's what I have to tell you, Socrates, about life under Cronus; our present life, which is supposed to be under Zeus,* you know about at first hand. But are you able, or are you inclined, to decide which of the two ways of life makes people happier?

YOUNG SOCRATES: No, I can't.

STRANGER: Shall I find a criterion for assessing them?

YOUNG SOCRATES: Yes, please.

STRANGER: As well as having so much spare time, Cronus' wards had the ability to communicate with animals as well as human beings. This being so, the crucial issue is whether
c they used all these advantages of theirs for philosophical purposes. If they entered into discussions with animals as well as with one another, and if, whenever they found that a given species had a particular talent, they tried to learn in what unique way it could add to their understanding, then it's an easy decision: they were infinitely happier than people nowadays. However, if they stuffed themselves with food and drink and had the kinds of conversation with one another and with the animal species that we hear about these days in our stories, then again, if I may tell you what
d I think, it's easy to decide the issue. Still, let's drop this topic for the time being, until we come across someone who can give us reliable information about which of the two attitudes people in those days held about knowledge and which of the two purposes they made conversation serve. We'd better turn to the reasons for bringing up this myth of ours, so that we can make progress and complete the next phase of our argument.

Eventually, this whole set-up had lasted as long as it was meant to and there had to be a change. In particular, the

whole earth-born race had been used up, since every soul e
had fulfilled its quota of incarnations and had fallen to
earth as seed as often as had been ordained for it. Then the
helmsman of the universe released the tiller, so to speak, and
withdrew to his vantage-point, and both fate and its innate
longing made the universe start to move backwards. As
soon as all the gods who had deputized for the supreme
deity in the various domains of his kingdom realized what
was happening, they too released their sections of the
cosmos.

The universe, driven by impulses whose endings and 273a
beginnings were opposed, recoiled and crashed against itself.
This caused a series of immense shocks to pass through it,
and these shocks annihilated, yet again, all kinds of living
creatures. Subsequently, once enough time had passed, the
chaos and disturbance ended, the shocks died down, and the
universe was at peace. Normality and order were restored
to its course. It had governance and responsibility for itself
and all its parts, and did its best to remember the injunc- b
tions it had been given by its father-creator. At first, it
carried out his commands quite exactly, but later—because
at least some of its components were material—some
precision was lost, since before attaining its current ordered
form as the cosmos, materiality (a primordial and inherent
aspect of the universe) was thoroughly steeped in disorder.
For all the good there is in the universe stems from the
constructor of the universe, whereas cruelty and injustice,
in so far as they are features of the universe, stem from
the disorderly condition it used to be in; the universe would c
not include these qualities, nor would it breed them in its
creatures, had it never been in that condition.

While the universe was under the helmsman's influence,
then, it used to engender little bad and plenty of good in the
creatures it maintained within its boundaries. But then
the helmsman departs. In the period immediately following
the release, the universe manages everything very well, but

as time goes by it gets more and more forgetful. Then that primeval disharmony gains the upper hand and, towards the end of this period, the universe runs riot and implants a blend of little good and plenty of the opposite, until it comes close to destroying itself and everything in it.

d

When the god who organized the universe sees the dreadful state it has got itself in by this stage, he is concerned. He doesn't want to see it swept away and wrecked by the storms of chaos, to founder in the infinite sea of dissimilarity. And that is why he resumes his place at the helm and puts it back on a new tack, away from the corruption and decomposition it had been steering towards under its own impulse in the preceding cycle; that is why he organizes it again, corrects it, and makes it immortal and ageless once more.

e

There is nothing more to be said on this, but if we take up the earlier part of the tale, it will help us in our attempt to understand kingship. Once the universe had been set on the path towards the way things are today, the process of ageing again came to a standstill and produced another series of extraordinary phenomena—the opposite of those which had happened before. Creatures which were so small that they were just about to vanish began to grow; bodies which had just been born from the ground with grey hair died and returned to the earth. What was happening to the universe as a whole was being repeated and reproduced in the changes everything was undergoing, and in particular the processes of pregnancy, birth, and child-rearing conformed of necessity to the general pattern. Creatures could no longer develop inside the earth as a result of various elements coming together and combining, so it was ordained that all the constituent parts of the universe should do their best to propagate and give birth and maintain their offspring by themselves, because this conformed to and was part of the same tendency which ordained that the universe as a whole should be responsible for its own course.

274a

We have now reached the point we were aiming at all b
along in this tale. It would be a long, complicated matter
to explain how and why all the other animals changed, but
it won't take long to describe what happened to human
beings, and that will be more relevant to our purposes.
Now, we had previously been maintained by a deity,
whose flock we were, but then this deity's supervision was
removed. At the same time, most animals became wild,
because they were innately fierce, and started to prey on
the weak, and now defenceless, human race. In these early
days, human beings had not yet developed their tools and c
skills; they had been accustomed to being maintained without having to do anything themselves, but now they were
deprived of that and they didn't yet know how to provide
for themselves, since no need had ever forced them to learn
in the past how to do so. As a result of all this, they were in a
very bad way indeed. That is why the gods gave us the gifts
we hear about in the ancient tales, along with the necessary
education and training—fire from Prometheus, the crafts
from Hephaestus and the goddess who shares his skill,* d
seeds and plants from others. This is the origin of everything which contributes towards the totality of human life,
following the event I recounted a moment ago when we
were deprived of divine supervision and had to start fending
for ourselves and being responsible for ourselves, just as the
universe as a whole did. In conformity and in keeping with
the rhythms of the universe, we swing for all time this way
and that in our lives and in the means of our birth. Anyway,
I think we should end the myth there and start to put it to e
work.*

10. ATLANTIS AND THE ANCIENT CITY OF ATHENS

(*Timaeus* 20d–25d; *Critias* 108e–121c)

Timaeus and *Critias* were in all probability the first two parts of a trilogy. *Critias*, however, was left unfinished, and the last part of the trilogy, whose title may have been *Hermocrates*, was not even begun. *Timaeus* opens with a scene describing a banquet, a *sumposion* in Greek. Literally *sumposion* means 'a drinking together', but the Greek banquet is an orchestrated event whose key entertainment element is the conversation of the participants, not a chaotic drinking party (although it may occasionally end up like this). The opening scene of *Timaeus* describes the second day of an ongoing banquet. The day before Socrates was *sumposiarchos*, that is, the leader of the banquet, and he entertained his guests—Timaeus, Critias, Hermocrates, and an unnamed participant—with a discourse about the ideal state. Today it is their turn to entertain him.

First, however, Socrates summarizes the discourse he gave 'yesterday' (which covers many points of *Republic*'s extensive discussion about the ideal state, including a scheme for education in the ideal state). Then he tells his banquet fellows that he is now seized with a desire of seeing the state he imagined in some action, such as war, which will point out its superiority more clearly. And what a coincidence! 'As soon as we arrived yesterday at the guest-chamber of Critias, with whom we are staying,' says Hermocrates, 'and even while we were on the way there, this was exactly the topic of our discussion, and Critias told us an ancient story' (20c). This story, Critias claims, was brought to Greece by Solon, who heard it from an Egyptian priest, and it is 'a fact and not a fiction' (26e). And it may satisfy Socrates' desire to see his ideal state in action, for it tells how the ancient city of Athens engaged in war with the terrifying and mighty Atlantis, and how its political superiority helped it win the war. Socrates is of course eager to hear the story, but Critias gives him only a summary of it (20d–25d), saying that the feast they prepared for him is not confined to this story.

First Timaeus, an astronomer who 'has made the nature of the universe his special study', will speak about 'the generation of the world and the creation of man' (27a). Then Critias will follow; his discourse will, as it were, receive the men brought forth by Timaeus' speech, give to some of them the education praised by Socrates in his discourse on the ideal state, and make them the citizens of the brave ancient city of Athens recovered from oblivion by the story Solon heard in Egypt. Socrates gives his approval, and Timaeus proceeds with his discourse, a fascinating cosmology that goes down to the end of *Timaeus*. This cosmology, held for centuries as Plato's greatest philosophical achievement, features a Demiurge (that is, a craftsman) who frames the soul and body of the universe and man from pre-existing matter (*passim*), which is dominated by an inner impulse towards disorder called 'necessity' (48a).

Critias opens with a brief discussion about the merits of Timaeus' discourse, and then goes on with a detailed version of Critias' story about Atlantis and the ancient city of Athens (108d–121c). Of *Critias*, however, we have only the first pages, and we do not know why Plato stopped in the middle of it. But the story it tells is not unfinished: we know how it ends from Critias' own summary, which occurs at the beginning of *Timaeus*. The question of the sources of Critias' story (if any) has divided Platonists from ancient times. The lack of historical evidence for a city such as Atlantis, however, as well as Plato's inclination towards the use of fiction for philosophical purposes, seems to suggest that he invented it.

The universe and human nature (Timaeus' discourse), society (Socrates' summary of the discourse he gave the day before), and history (Critias' story about the ancient city of Athens and Atlantis)—these are the main themes of *Timaeus* and *Critias*. They are all united by the same motif: the relation between what is rational (the Demiurge, the rulers of the ideal state, the ancient city of Athens) and what is non-rational (necessity, the citizens that have to be ruled, Atlantis). But while the Demiurge persuaded Necessity to obey his rational plans, the rulers of the ideal state impose their regime upon their fellow citizens, and the evil Atlantis had to be conquered. The world we live in and our own nature, Plato seems to be saying, is grounded on co-operation between the rational and the non-rational, while our communal life and history always involves a confrontation between the two. Why? Because, one may venture to say, the Demiurge who created the universe did not choose to be men's shepherd. The Demiurge 'was good, and the good can never have any jealousy of anything. And being free of jealousy, he desired that all things should be as like himself as they could be' (*Ti.* 29e–30a). Thus the universe he created is said to be the best possible universe (92c). But, after he completed his creation, the Demiurge seems to retire and not have any interest in guiding the communal life of men. Our reason— which is the divine element in us (being framed by the Demiurge himself, as it is said in *Timaeus*)—is the only thing that could make our communal life get closer to a divine ruling. That is why every-thing in the Platonic attempt to imagine a better state, in *Republic* or *Laws*, is centred upon reason; see, for instance, *L.* 713e–714a: 'When a community is ruled not by God but by a mortal human being, its members have no refuge from evil and misery. We should do our utmost . . . to order our private households and our public societies alike in obedience to the immortal element within us, giving the name of law to the regulations prescribed by reason.' Which seems to imply that Plato—in spite of claiming that the traditional Greek gods were at first the herdsmen of men (cf. *Criti.* 109b)—perceived human society as being already deserted by gods, left with nothing but human reason to rely on.

C.P.

———

Timaeus 20d–25d

20d CRITIAS: All right, then. Socrates, you are about to hear a story which, for all its strangeness, is absolutely true, with its truth affirmed by Solon, the wisest of the seven

e sages.* Now, Solon was a relative of my great-grandfather Dropides, and the two of them were very close, as Solon himself often says in his verses.* Dropides told the story to my grandfather Critias and the old man used to repeat it to us in his turn. He used to tell us that there were impressive and remarkable deeds performed long ago by Athens which had been obliterated by time and the destruction of human life.* One of these exploits was especially impressive, and 21a recalling it now will be a suitable way not only to pay you what we owe you, but also to praise the goddess with the kind of truth-telling she deserves in a hymn, so to speak, on the occasion of her festival.*

SOCRATES: That sounds good. So Critias told you, on Solon's authority, of a deed performed long ago by our city, and he said that it was no mere story but an actual event. What was this deed?

CRITIAS: I shall tell you. I heard the ancient tale from a man who was no youngster himself, since Critias was, by his own reckoning, getting on for 90 years old by then, while I was b 10 at the most. It was, as it happens, the Koureotis of the Apatouria,* and the usual children's event, which happens every time the festival is held, took place then too—which is to say that our fathers instituted a recitation contest. Various works by various poets featured in the recital, but many of the children sang Solon's verses because they were new at that time.

One of the members of our phratry* remarked (either because he really believed it at the time or just to please Critias) that Solon was not only a great sage in general, but c as a poet was more independent than anyone else.* The old man, as I remember clearly, was delighted with this and said with a smile: 'Yes, Amynander, and if only he had not taken up poetry merely as a hobby, but had worked as seriously at it as other poets do! And I wish that he had finished the story he brought back from Egypt, and hadn't been forced to neglect it by the feuding and other evils he found here when he got home. If he had, I dare say that he would have become more famous as a poet than Hesiod, Homer, and all d the rest.' 'What story was that, Critias?' asked Amynander. 'It was about our city's most impressive achievement ever,' Critias replied, 'one which deserves to be better known than any other, but time and the destruction of the people

involved have prevented the story from surviving until now.'
'Do please tell us it from start to finish,' said Amynander.
'What was this true story that Solon told? How did he come
to hear it? Who told it to him?'

e   'In Egypt,' Critias said, 'around that part of the Delta
where the Nile forks at its crown, there is a district called
the Saïtic province, where the largest city is Saïs, which
was also the birthplace of King Amasis.* The founder of
this city was a deity whose Egyptian name is Neïth, though
in Greek, according to the Egyptians, she is Athena. The
inhabitants claim to be very pro-Athenian and somehow to
be related to us. Solon said that he was heaped with honours
on his arrival there,* but the main thing he said was that,
22a   when he once questioned those priests who were experts in
history about the past, he discovered how almost completely
ignorant about such matters he and every other Greek was.
Once, he said, he wanted to draw them into a discussion
of ancient history, and so he launched into an account of
the earliest events known here: he began to talk about
Phoroneus, who is said to have been the first man, and
b   Niobe; he told the story of Deucalion and Pyrrha and of
how they survived the flood, and traced the genealogies
of their descendants; and he tried to calculate their dates
by recording the number of years since the events he was
talking about.*

'Then one of the priests, a very old man, said: "Solon,
Solon, you Greeks never grow up; there isn't an old man
among you."

'"What do you mean?" said Solon in response.

'"You are all mentally immature," the priest replied. "You
have no ancient tradition to imbue your minds with old
beliefs and with understanding aged by time. I shall tell you
c   why this is so. The human race has often been destroyed
in various ways, and will be in the future too. Fire and
water have been responsible for the most devastating catastrophes, but there have also been countless causes of briefer

disasters. For instance, you have a story of how Phaethon, scion of the Sun, once harnessed his father's chariot, but was incapable of driving it along the path his father took and so burnt up everything on the surface of the earth and was himself killed by a thunderbolt. This story has the form of a fable, but it alludes to a real event*—the deviation* of the d heavenly bodies that go around the earth and the periodic destruction at long intervals of the surface of the earth by a massive conflagration.

'"When this happens, all those people who live in mountainous regions and in places that are high and dry are far more likely to die than those who live by rivers and the sea. The Nile, which is invariably our saviour, saves us at these times from disaster by being released.* On the other hand, when the gods purge the earth with a flood of water, it is the herdsmen and shepherds in the mountains who are saved, while the inhabitants of your cities are swept into the e sea by the rivers. In our land, however, water never flows on to our fields from above*—it doesn't on these occasions and it doesn't at other times either—but instead its nature is such that it rises up from below.*

'"This explains why the legends preserved here are the most ancient, although in actual fact the human race is continuous, in larger or smaller numbers, everywhere in the world where there is neither excessive cold nor excessive 23a heat to prevent it. But every impressive or important or otherwise outstanding event we hear about, whether it happens in your part of the world or here or elsewhere, has from ancient times been written down here in the temples and preserved. However, what happens in your part of the world and elsewhere is that no sooner have you been equipped at any time with literacy and the other resources of city life when once again, after the usual interval, a heavenly flood pours down on you like a plague and leaves only those who are illiterate and uncivilized. As a result, b you once again regain your childlike state of ignorance about things which happened both here and in your part of the world in ancient times.

'"For instance, Solon, the genealogies you just went through for people from your part of the world hardly differ from childish tales. In the first place, you remember just the one flood when there have been many in earlier times, and in addition you are unaware that the finest and most heroic race in all humankind once existed in your land. You and all your current fellow citizens are the descendants of what little of their stock remained, but none of you realizes it, because for many generations the survivors died without leaving a written record. But in fact there was a time, Solon, before the greatest and most destructive flood, when the city which is now Athens not only excelled in warfare, but was also outstandingly well governed in all respects. The finest achievements and the finest political institutions we have ever heard of on earth are attributed to it."

'Solon told us of his astonishment at this and said that he begged the priests with all the determination he could muster to give him a detailed and thorough account of those citizens of long ago. And the priest replied: "I'll do so gladly, Solon, not just for your sake and for Athens, but especially for the sake of the goddess who is the patron, nurse, and governess of both our cities. Your city was founded first, when the goddess received your rootstock from Earth and Hephaestus, and ours was founded a thousand years later.* The written records in our temples give the figure of 8,000 years as the age of our system, so it is citizens who lived 9,000 years ago whose customs and whose finest achievement I shall briefly explain to you. You and I will consult the written records on some future occasion, when we have time, and go through them thoroughly and in detail.

'"It's worth comparing their way of life with ours here, because you will find many current instances here of customs that used in those days to obtain in your part of the

102

world.* First, the priestly caste is separated off from all the rest, and next you'll find that each set of craftsmen—such as herdsmen, hunters, and farmers—works independently, without involvement in anyone else's craft. Then I'm sure b you've noticed how the warrior caste here is set apart from all the others, and that it is a legal requirement that they should focus exclusively on military matters. Moreover, their weaponry consists of shields and spears, which we were the first in Asia* to adopt, following the example of the goddess,* just as you did first in those regions where you Greeks live. Then again, where intellectual matters are concerned, I'm sure you can see how much attention our way of life here has devoted to the thorough study of the universe, until on the basis of these divine principles we have discovered everything relevant to human affairs, up to and c including divination and the medical skills necessary for health, and have acquired all the other branches of knowledge which follow from these principles.

'"The system and arrangement I have been describing from those days was in fact first instituted and founded by the goddess among your people. She chose the region in which you had been born because she noticed how the temperate climate there would produce men of outstanding intelligence.* Because the goddess is fond of both war and wisdom, she chose this region as the one which would pro- d duce men who would most closely resemble herself and founded a city there first. And so your people began to live there and to rely on customs such as those I have described. In fact, you had an even better system of government than ours and there was no people on earth which came close to your all-round excellence—which is hardly surprising since you were the offspring and the wards of gods.

'"Many of your city's exploits which have been written down here are impressive enough to excite admiration, but there is one above all which stands out for its importance and courage. Our documents record how your city once e halted an enormous force which was marching insolently against not just the whole of Europe, but Asia as well, from its base beyond Europe in the Atlantic Ocean. I should mention that in those days the ocean there was navigable, since there was an island in front of the strait which, I've heard you say, your people call the Pillars of Heracles.* The island was bigger than both Asia and Libya combined, and travellers in those days used it to gain access to the remaining islands, from which they could travel over to

25a   any point of the mainland opposite which surrounds that genuine sea.* You see, everything this side of the strait we mentioned is like a harbour with a narrow entrance, whereas that is the true sea and the land which completely surrounds it truly deserves the name 'mainland'.

'"On this island of Atlantis a great and remarkable dynasty had arisen, which ruled the whole island, many of the other islands, and parts of the mainland too. They also

b   governed some of the lands here inside the strait too—Libya up to Egypt and Europe up to Etruria.* Once upon a time, then, they combined their forces and set out *en masse* to try to enslave in one swoop your part of the world, and ours, and all the territory this side of the strait. This was the occasion, Solon, when the capacity of your city, its courage and strength, were revealed for all to see;* its bravery and military expertise made it stand out from all others. At

c   first it was the leader of the Greek cause, and then later, abandoned by everyone else and compelled to stand alone, it came to the very brink of disaster, but it overcame the invaders and erected a trophy, thereby preventing the enslavement of those who remained unenslaved and unhesitatingly liberating all the rest of us who lived this side of the boundaries of Heracles.

'"Some time later appalling earthquakes and floods

d   occurred, and in the course of a single, terrible day and night the whole fighting force of your city sank all at once beneath the earth, and the island of Atlantis likewise sank beneath the sea and vanished. That is why the sea there cannot now be navigated or explored; the mud which the island left behind as it settled lies a little below the surface* and gets in the way."'

Critias 108e–121c

'Let's recall, first, that in all nine thousand years* have passed 108e since war was declared between between those who lived beyond and all those who lived within the Pillars of Heracles. This is the war whose course I shall now describe. It is said that one side was led right through to the end of the fighting by Athens, while the other side was commanded by the kings of Atlantis—an island which, we said, was once larger than Libya and Asia, though by now earthquakes have caused it to sink and it has left behind unnavigable mud which obstructs 109a those who sail out there into the ocean.* As our tale unfolds, so to speak, along its course, there will be opportunities to reveal details of the many non-Greek peoples and all the Greek communities that existed then, but to begin with we must start with an account of the resources and the political systems of the Athenians of the time and their opponents in the war. And of the two sides, we should give preference to an account of affairs here in Athens.

'Once upon a time the gods divided the whole earth among b themselves, region by region. There were no disputes involved;* after all, it makes no sense for the gods not to know what is appropriate to each of them and, since they do have such knowledge, it is illogical to believe that they would dispute claims and try to gain what is properly suited to some-one else. So each gained by just allotment what belonged to him, established communities in his lands, and, having done so, began to look after us, his property and creatures, as a shepherd does his flocks,* with the difference that they did not use physical means of compulsion. Shepherds use blows as c they tend to their flocks, but the gods focused on that part of each creature which makes it most easy to direct, like helms-men steering from the prow; they took hold of its mind, employed the rudder of persuasion as they saw fit, and in this way guided and led every mortal creature as a whole.

'As a result of the allotment various gods gained various regions to govern, but Hephaestus and Athena (who are very similar in nature, not just because they are brother and sister, with a common father, but also because their love of wisdom and of craft give them the same goals) gained Athens here as their common allocation, since the nature of the dis-

d trict was such that it was suitable for courage and intelligence.* So they created men of courage who were born from the ground* and implanted in their minds the plan of their political system.

'Although the names of these first Athenians have been preserved, their achievements have been obliterated by the destruction of their successors and the long passage of time. I have already mentioned* the reason for this: those who survived on each occasion were illiterate mountain-dwellers who had heard only the names of the rulers of the land and knew hardly anything about their achievements. They were

e happy to name their children after their predecessors, but were unaware of their acts of courage and their customs, except for the occasional obscure rumour about this or that. For many generations they and their children were short of essentials

110a and this problem was what occupied their minds and con-versations, rather than events of the distant past. After all, story-telling and enquiring about the past arrive in com-munities along with leisure, when and only when they see that some people have been adequately supplied with the necessities of life.

'Anyway, this is how the names but not the achievements of those men of old came to be preserved. My evidence for saying this is that, according to Solon, the account those priests gave of the war of that time included not only most of the names of Cecrops, Erechtheus, Erichthonius, Erysichthon, and the

other predecessors of Theseus, but also a great many of the b
achievements that are attributed to each of their names;
and the same went, he said, for their wives. Moreover, as for
the way the goddess is portrayed, Solon said that in those days
military training was undertaken by women as well as by men,
and that it was in accordance with this practice that people in
those days began to display the goddess in armour. It was a
token of the fact that all gregarious animals, female and male, c
have been equally equipped by their natures to practise the
virtue peculiar to their species.*

'In those days most of the inhabitants of this land—most
classes of citizens—were occupied with the crafts and with
agriculture, but the warrior class, which from the very
beginning had been separated off by godlike men,* lived apart.
They had everything that was appropriate for their sustenance
and training, and although they owned no private property
and regarded everything as held in common by them all, they d
did not expect the rest of their fellow citizens to provide them
with anything more than an adequate supply of food. In fact,
their way of life was in all respects the same as that described
yesterday for our imaginary guardians.*

'Then again, the old stories about our land are reliable
and true: above all, in those days its border was formed by
the Isthmus and, in relation to the rest of the mainland, our
territory extended as far as the hills of Cithaeron and Parnes
and went down to the coast with Oropus on the right and e
the Asopus forming the border on the left.* There was no soil
to compare to ours anywhere in the world, which is why the
territory was capable in those days of supporting a large
number of soldiers who were exempt from working the
land.* There is convincing proof of how good the soil was: the
remnant of it that still exists is a match for any soil in its ability
to produce a good yield of any crop and in the rich pasturage it
provides for all sorts of animals. But in those days the soil 111a
produced crops in vast quantities; they were not just of high
quality.

'Why should we trust this picture? Why are we right to call the soil of modern Attica a remnant of the soil of those days? Attica is nothing but a headland, so to speak, jutting far out into the sea from the rest of the mainland, and it is surrounded by a sea-bed which drops off close to shore to a considerable depth. So since there have been many devastating floods in the course of the 9,000-year interval between then and now,

b the soil washed down from the highlands in all these years and during these disasters does not form any considerable pile of sediment, as it does elsewhere, but is constantly rolled down into the depths, where it vanishes. Just as on the small islands,* what remains now is, compared with those days, like the skeleton of a body wasted by disease: the soil has rolled away—or at least as much of it as is rich and soft—and only the thin body of the land remains.

'In those days, however, the land was intact and had high

c mounds instead of mountains, what we now call the Stony Plains were filled with rich soil, and the mountains were covered with dense forests (of which there are traces even now). Nowadays some of our mountains sustain only bees, but not long ago trees from there were cut as roof timbers for very substantial buildings, and the roofs are still sound. Cultivated trees grew tall and plentiful and the soil bore limitless fodder for our flocks and herds. Moreover, the ground benefited

d from the rain sent each year by Zeus and didn't lose it, as it does nowadays with the water flowing off the bare ground and into the sea. Instead, because the ground had plenty of soil to absorb moisture, it stored the rain on a layer of impermeable clay, let the water flow down from the high ground into the low ground of every region, and so provided abundant springs to feed streams and rivers. Even now there are still shrines, left over from the old days, at the sites of former springs, as tokens of the truth of this account of the land.

e 'So much for the characteristics of the land in general. It was ordered as well as you might expect, given that the farmers were true farmers (that is, they were specialists at their job, and were endowed with noble aims and natural ability) and given that they had outstandingly good soil to work with, plenty of water, and a perfectly tempered climate from the skies above. As for the state of the town in those days, in the first place the Acropolis was different from now, since by 112a now it has suffered from the effects of a single night of torrential rain, which washed away the soil and left the Acropolis bare, thanks not only to an appalling deluge—the third destruction by water before the one that took place in the time of Deucalion*—but to earthquakes too. Before then, the Acropolis extended from the Eridanus to the Ilissus, included the Pnyx, and had the Lycabettus as its border on the side opposite the Pnyx;* and the entire Acropolis was covered in soil and was almost all level. Outside the Acropolis, under its flanks, were the dwellings of the craftsmen and those farmers b who worked the nearby land.

'The top of the Acropolis had been settled by the warriors, who lived all by themselves around the temple of Athena and Hephaestus, and had also enclosed the heights within a single wall, like the garden of a single house. They lived in communal houses on the northern side of the Acropolis, they had constructed messes to be shared by all in cold weather, and they had provided themselves with everything that was in keeping with their communal institutions—everything in the way of c buildings and temples, that is, not gold and silver, for which they never had any use. In pursuit of the mean between extravagance and dependence, they built moderate houses in which they and their descendants could grow old and which they could bequeath to others just like themselves. As for the southern side, when, as you would expect, they left their gardens, gymnasia, and messes in the summer, they used this side for these functions. There was a single spring in the area of the present Acropolis, but it has been clogged up by earthquakes, so that now there is only a trickle of water around the d present hill; but in those days it supplied everyone with plenty of water and kept a constant temperature throughout the year.

'This was the manner of their lives. As guardians of their own fellow citizens and of all other Greeks, who were their willing subjects,* they did their best to ensure that at any given time there were among them the same number of men and
e women—around twenty thousand—who were already or were still capable of fighting. This, then, was what the Athenians were like in those days, and their way of life was more or less as I have said. They equitably managed their own affairs and those of Greece, they were renowned throughout Europe and Asia for their physical beauty and for their many outstanding mental qualities, and their fame surpassed that of all their contemporaries.

'Now let's turn to their opponents in the war. Assuming I can remember it, I shall now reveal to you, because friends hold all things in common, what I was told in my childhood about what they were like and how their way of life evolved.
113a But first, there's a small point I should explain before telling the tale, otherwise you might be surprised at constantly hearing Greek names applied to non-Greek people. I'll tell you how this came about. Solon was planning to create a poetic version of the tale, and so he asked about the meanings of the names and found that the Egyptians who had first written the story down had translated them into their own language. So he did the same: he referred back to the sense of each
b name and adapted it to our language before committing it to writing. And it is his written version which once belonged to my grandfather and is now in my possession. I studied the manuscript carefully when I was young. So if you hear Greek-sounding names, don't be surprised: you now know why.* Anyway, it's a long story and it began somewhat as follows.

'As I said earlier, the gods parcelled out the entire world among themselves, allocated themselves larger or smaller
c territories, and established their own shrines and sacrificial rituals. Poseidon gained the island of Atlantis as his province and he settled there the children borne for him by a mortal woman in a certain part of the island. To be specific, halfway

along the coastline there was a plain which is said to have been unsurpassable in its beauty and adequately fertile too. Close to the plain and halfway along its extent, about fifty stades distant from the coast, there was a hill of no great prominence. There lived on this hill a man who was one of the original earth-born men of the land. He was called Evenor and he lived with his d wife, Leucippe. They had just the one child, a daughter called Cleito. When the girl reached the age for marriage, both her mother and her father died, but Poseidon, who had come to desire her, made her his concubine. He gave the hill where she lived secure defences by breaking it off from the surrounding land and creating increasingly large concentric rings, alternately of land and water, around it. Two of the rings were of land, three of water, and he made them equidistant from the centre, as if he had taken the middle of the island as the pivot of a lathe.* And so the island became inaccessible to e others, because in those days ships and sailing had not yet been invented.*

'Poseidon, as a god, easily organized the central island. Once he had fetched up two underground springs—one warm, the other flowing cold from its source—and caused all kinds of food to grow in sufficient abundance from the soil, he fathered and reared five pairs of twin sons. Then he divided the entire island of Atlantis into ten parts. He gave the first-born of the eldest twins his mother's home and the plot 114a of land around it, which was larger and more fertile than anywhere else, and made him king of all his brothers, while giving each of the others many subjects and plenty of land to rule over.

'He named all his sons. To the eldest, the king, he gave the name from which the names of the whole island and the ocean are derived—that is, the ocean was called the Atlantic because the name of the first king was Atlas. To his twin, the one who b was born next, who gained as his allotment the edge of the island which is closest to the Pillars of Heracles and faces the land which is now called the territory of Gadeira after him, he gave a name which in Greek would be Eumelus, though in the local language it was Gadeirus, and so this must be the origin of the name of Gadeira.* He called the next pair of twins Ampheres and Evaemon; he named the elder of the

c third pair Mneseus and the younger one Autochthon; of the fourth pair the eldest was called Elasippus and the younger one Mestor; in the case of the fifth pair, he called the first-born Azaes and the second-born Diaprepes. So all his sons and their descendants lived there for many generations, and in addition to ruling over numerous other islands in the ocean, they also, as I said before,* governed all the land this side of the Pillars up to Egypt and Etruria.

d 'Atlas' family flourished in numbers and prestige. In each generation the eldest was king and passed the kingship on to the eldest of his offspring. In this way the dynasty survived for many generations and they grew enormously rich, with more wealth than anyone from any earlier royal line and more than anyone later would easily gain either; and they were supplied with everything they needed for life in the city and throughout the rest of their territory too. Their empire brought them many goods from abroad, but the island by

e itself provided them with most of the necessities of life. In the first place, they had everything, solid or fusible,* that could be mined from the ground, and in fact in many parts of the island there was dug up from the ground something which is now no more than a name, although in those days it was more than just a name and was second in value only to gold— orichalc.* Second, woodland produced plenty of every kind of timber that builders might need for their labours and bore enough food for both wild and domesticated animals. In fact, there were even large numbers of elephants there, because there was ample grazing for all creatures—not just for those

115a whose habitats were marshes and lakes and rivers, or again for those that lived in mountains or on the plains, but equally for this creature too, the largest and most voracious in the world.

'Third, everything aromatic the earth produces today in the way of roots or shoots or shrubs or gums exuded by flowers or fruits was produced and supported by the island then. Fourth, as for cultivated crops—both the dry sort (that is, our staple and all the others we use as foodstuffs, which we collectively call 'pulses') and the arboreal sort (not only the sources of our b drink and food and oil, but also the produce of fruit-bearing trees which, though hard to store, exists for the sake of our amusement and our pleasure, and also all those things we offer a man who is full up as an enjoyable dessert to relieve his satiety*)—all these things were in those days produced in vast quantities and at a remarkably high level of excellence by that sacred, sun-drenched island.

'Enriched by all these agricultural products, they set about building shrines, royal mansions, harbours, and shipyards, and c organized the whole of their territory along the following lines. The first thing they did was build bridges across the rings of water surrounding the ancient mother-city, to create a road to and from the palace. The palace was the very first thing they had built in the place where Poseidon and their ancestors had lived, and it was passed down from generation to generation, with each new king embellishing what was already embellished and trying as best he could to outdo his predecessors, until d they had created a building of astonishing size and beauty.

'What they did first was dig a canal from the sea to the outermost ring. The canal was three plethra wide, a hundred feet deep, and fifty stades long,* and with a mouth wide enough for the largest ships it allowed vessels to sail from the sea to the outermost ring and to use it as a harbour. Moreover, e at the points where they had built the bridges they opened up gaps in the intermediate rings of land wide enough to allow a single warship to sail through from one ring of water to another, and they roofed these canals over so as to create an underground sailing passage below,* for the banks of the rings of land were high enough above the level of the water to allow them to do this.

'The largest ring of water—the one into which the sea had been channelled—was three stades wide, and the next ring of land was the same size. Of the second pair, the ring of water was two stades wide, and the ring of land was again the same size as the preceding ring of water. The ring of water which immediately surrounded the central island was a stade in width, while the island (where the palace was) had a diameter of five stades.

116a

'They surrounded the central island and the rings of land and the bridges (which were one plethron wide) on both sides with a stone wall, and built towers and gates on the bridges at each side, at the points where there were the passages for the water. They quarried the stone (some white, some black, and some red) from underneath the perimeter of the central island and from under the outside and inside of the rings of land, so that at the same time they hollowed out internal, double-sided docks, roofed over by the actual rock. They made some of their buildings plain, but to avoid monotony they patterned others by combining stones, which gave the buildings a naturally pleasant appearance. They covered the entire circuit of the wall around the outermost ring with a paste, so to speak, of bronze; they smeared a layer of melted tin on the wall of the inner ring; and for the wall around the acropolis itself they used orichalc, which gleamed like fire.*

b

c

'The palace inside the acropolis was fitted out as follows. In the very centre was a sacrosanct shrine dedicated to Cleito and Poseidon, surrounded by a low wall of gold. This was the spot where they had originally conceived and fathered the ten kings. It was here too, in this shrine, that in an annual ritual each of the ten kings received first-fruits from all the ten regions. There was a temple of Poseidon there, which was a stade long and three plethra wide, and its height was aesthetically proportionate with these base measurements. There was something non-Greek about the appearance of the temple.* Outside, it was entirely covered with silver except for the acroteria,* which were gold. Inside, the entire surface of

d

the ceiling was ivory decorated with gold, silver, and orichalc, and all the walls, pillars, and pavements were covered with orichalc. They set up a golden statue there of the god standing on a chariot with a team of six winged horses, tall enough to e touch the roof with his head. He was surrounded by another hundred golden statues of Nereids on dolphins (in those days people thought there were this many Nereids*), and the temple also held many other statues, which had been dedicated by private individuals.

'Outside, the temple was surrounded by golden statues of all the ten kings and their wives, and there were numerous other substantial dedications, given by both the kings and private individuals from the city itself and also from the foreign territories of their empire. The altar conformed to this structure in size and workmanship, and the palace was equally 117a in keeping not just with the size of the empire, but also with the beauty of the shrine.

'They drew their water from the two springs (one of cold and the other of warm water), each of which was fantastically well suited to its function in respect of the taste and the quality of the water, which it produced in generous quantities. They surrounded the springs with buildings and with copses of suitable trees, and also with pools, some of which they left open to the air, while they protected with roofs those which b were used in the winter as warm baths. There were separate sets of pools—some for the royal families, some for private citizens, others for women, and yet others for horses and other yoke-animals—and each pool was organized in the appropriate fashion. Any water which overflowed was channelled to the grove of Poseidon, where all the various species of trees grew to be beautiful and extraordinarily tall thanks to the fertility of the soil, and was then conducted to the rings beyond the island by pipes beside the bridges.

'Numerous shrines, sacred to a large number of gods, c had been built on these outer rings, and there were plenty of gardens and gymnasia there too. There were separate

exercise-grounds for men and for horses on each of the two islands formed by the rings and, above all, in the middle of the larger of the island-rings they had an area reserved as a hippodrome. The hippodrome was a stade wide and ran all the way around the ring, as a space dedicated to equestrian contests. Most of the bodyguards* lived on either side of
d the hippodrome, but the more trusted ones were assigned barracks on the smaller ring, closer to the citadel, and those who were exceptionally trustworthy were allowed to live in close proximity to the kings themselves within the citadel. The shipyards were filled with warships and with all the equipment they required, and everything was in a state of readiness.

'So much for the way the royal household was fitted out. Past the three external harbours a wall ran all around, starting
e at the sea, at a constant distance of fifty stades from the largest ring and its harbour, and completed its circuit at the point where it began, at the mouth of the canal by the sea. This whole area was crowded with a great many houses, and the canal and the largest harbour teemed with merchant ships and traders arriving from all over the world, in such large numbers that all day and all night long the place resounded with shouts and general uproar and noise.

'I have now pretty well covered the original account of the town and the ancient palace, and I had better try to tell you
118a what the character and arrangement of the rest of the land was like. To begin with, the whole region was said to be very high, with sheer cliffs along the coastline, but near the city there was nothing but a plain, which surrounded the city and was itself surrounded by mountains which stretched down to the sea. The plain was uniformly flat and basically oblong: it extended in one direction for 3,000 stades and inland across its centre 2,000 stades from the sea. This part of the island as a
b whole faced south* and was sheltered from the north winds. The mountains that surrounded the plain were celebrated in those days for their number, size, and beauty; there are no mountains today which come close to them in these respects.

There were in the mountains many wealthy villages with their rural populations; rivers, lakes, and meadows kept every species of tame and wild creature adequately supplied with food; and there was plenty of timber, of various types, which was more than sufficient for any kind of task and for every occasion.

'As a result of its nature, and of many years of engineering c by successive kings, the plain had taken on the following character. It was originally, as I said, largely rectangular, straight-sided, and oblong, but because it was not perfectly oblong they made it straight by surrounding it with a trench. The reported scale of this trench—its depth and width and length—was incredible: it is hard to believe that, on top of all their other engineering works, any work of human hands should be so huge. Still, I must tell you what I was told. It was excavated to a depth of a plethron, it was a stade wide all the way around, and its length, once the whole perimeter of d the plain had been excavated, was 10,000 stades. Streams descending from the mountains drained into it, and it made a complete circuit of the plain, so that it reached the city from both sides, and then the water was allowed to discharge into the sea. Inland from the city straight canals with a width of about 100 feet had been cut across the plain and debouched into the trench on the coastal side; each canal was 100 stades away from its neighbours. They used them not only to bring timber down to the city from the mountains, but also for the e ships with which they transported all the rest of their produce in its season. They also cut cross-channels at right angles to the canals, linking the canals to one another and to the city. They harvested their crops twice a year; in winter they relied on rain sent by Zeus, but in summer they diverted water from the canals to all their crops.

'As for the number of plain-dwelling men who were to be available for military service, it had been decreed that each plot (there were 60,000 in all, each ten by ten stades in area) was to provide one officer. There were, apparently, enormous 119a

numbers of men from the mountains and the rest of the land, and they were all assigned, region by region and village by village, to these plots and their officers. Each officer was instructed to supply for military use a sixth part of a war chariot (making a total of 10,000 chariots); two horses with
b riders; a pair of team horses without a chariot but with a light-armed soldier for dismounting, a charioteer for the pair of horses, and an on-board soldier to stand in front of the charioteer; two hoplites; two archers and the same number of slingers; three unarmed men to throw stones and the same number to throw javelins; and four sailors towards the total of 1,200 ships. This was how the royal city was organized militarily; the other nine cities did things differently, but it would take too long to explain their systems too.

c   'I shall now tell you what the original arrangements were for the wielding of power and authority. In his own particular region and where his own city was concerned, each of the ten kings had authority over the citizens and was more powerful than most of the laws, in the sense that he could punish and kill at whim. But among themselves authority and interaction were governed by the regulations of Poseidon, as bequeathed to them by tradition and by a stele of orichalc inscribed by
d their first ancestors and set up in the middle of the island in the shrine of Poseidon, where they used to meet, at intervals alternately of four and five years, so as to privilege neither odd nor even numbers. When they met, they would not only discuss matters of general interest, but also test one another, to see if any of them had infringed the regulations, and try any offender.

'When the time of trial arrived, the first thing they did was give assurances to one another, as follows. In the shrine of Poseidon there were consecrated bulls, and once the ten were alone they asked the god in their prayers to allow them to
e capture a sacrificial victim that would please him. They then took up sticks and nooses (not weapons of iron) and set about chasing the bulls, and once they had caught one they

led it to the stele and cut its throat above the head of the stele, so that its blood flowed over the inscription. In addition to the regulations the stele was inscribed with an oath which called down terrible curses on anyone who disobeyed the regulations.

'So when they had sacrificed the bull in their traditional manner and had burnt all its limbs, they prepared a mixing- 120a bowl of wine and threw in one clot of blood for each of them. The rest of the blood they poured into the fire, after thoroughly cleaning the stele. Next they used golden cups to scoop up some wine from the bowl, and while pouring a libation on to the fire they swore that they would adjudicate in conformity with the regulations inscribed on the stele, would punish any past infringements, would henceforth knowingly infringe none of the regulations, and would neither rule nor obey any ruler unless his injunctions accorded b with their father's regulations. Once he had committed himself and his descendants with this vow, each of the kings drank and then dedicated his cup to the god's shrine, before occupying himself with the feast* and whatever else he had to do. When darkness fell and the sacrificial fire had cooled down, they all put on gorgeous robes of dark blue, sat down in the dark on the ground by the charred remains of the sacrificial victim, and once they had extinguished every flame in c the shrine, they turned to the trial. They gave and received judgements for any infringement of the regulations and then, the following day, they inscribed their decisions on a golden tablet, which they dedicated in the shrine along with their robes as a memorial.

'There were many other rules and customs pertaining only to the prerogatives of each of the kings, but the most important points were that they should never take up arms against one another; that they should all resist any attempt to overthrow the royal family in any city; that, as their pre- decessors had, they should collectively debate any decisions d that were to be made about all matters such as warfare, while giving overall authority to the descendants of Atlas; and that no king should have the right to put any of his relatives to death, unless half of the ten agreed with his decision.

'So much for a description of the mighty power that existed in Atlantis in those days. It was this force that the god* mustered and brought against these regions here, and the account gave the following reason for his doing so. For e many generations, as long as Poseidon's nature was vigorous enough in them, they obeyed the laws and respected the divine element in themselves. Because the principles they had were true and thoroughly high-minded, and because they reacted with self-possession and intelligence to the vicissitudes of life and to one another, they looked down on everything except virtue, counted their prosperity as trivial, and easily bore the 121a burden, so to speak, of the mass of their gold and other possessions. They were not made drunk by the luxury their wealth afforded them and so they remained in control of themselves and never stumbled. As sober men do, they saw clearly that even prosperity is increased by the combination of mutual friendship and virtue—and that wealth declines and friendship is destroyed by materialistic goals and ambitions.

'As a result of this kind of reasoning and of the persistence of the divine nature within them, they thrived in all the ways I have described. But when the divine portion within them faded, as a result of constantly being diluted by large measures b of mortality, and their mortal nature began to predominate, they became incapable of bearing their prosperity and grew corrupt. Anyone with the eyes to see could mark the vileness of their behaviour as they destroyed the finest of their valuable possessions; but those who were blind to the life that truly leads to happiness regarded them as having finally attained the most desirable and enviable life possible, now that they were infected with immoral greed and power.

'Zeus, god of gods and legally ordained king, who did have the eyes to see such things, recognized the degenerate state c of their line and wished to punish them, and so to make their lives more graceful. He summoned all the gods to a meeting in the most awesome of his dwellings, which is located in the centre of the entire universe and so sees everything that is subject to generation. And when the gods had assembled, he said:*

EXPLANATORY NOTES

1. THE ORIGIN OF VIRTUE (*Protagoras* 320c–323a)

C. C. W. TAYLOR

320c ff. *Once upon a time there were just the gods*: the Greeks were familiar with two opposed accounts of human development: (*a*) that represented here, the naturalistic tradition, developed in the fifth century from traditional antecedents, of progress from primitive beginnings; (*b*) the older Hesiodic tradition of progressive decline from an original state of innocence. Plato's own theory (*Stm.* 273–4, *Ti.* 72–3, *Criti.* 110–12, *L.* 3. 676–82) combines elements of both traditions.

There has been much discussion of the question whether Protagoras' defence is based on an actual work of his (see W. K. C. Guthrie, *A History of Greek Philosophy*, iii, part 2 (Cambridge: Cambridge University Press, 1969), 64 n. 1). In view of the considerable interest in the fifth century in the origins of civilization (ibid. 60–84 and C. H. Kahn, 'The Origins of Social Contract Theory in the Fifth Century B.C.', in G. B. Kerferd, ed., *The Sophists and their Legacy* (*Hermes* Einzelschriften 44; Wiesbaden: Franz Steiner Verlag, 1981), 92–108), and in view of the fact that the list of titles of works attributed to Protagoras includes one 'On the original state of things' (Diogenes Laertius 9. 55), it is perfectly plausible that it is. On the other hand, nothing in the dialogue indicates that Protagoras' story might be familiar to his audience. In reply to Socrates' first objection, namely that the Athenians think that there are no experts on how to run the city, Protagoras argues that, on the contrary, they and everyone else regard all citizens as experts in that field. He supports this by giving, in the story, an account of the nature of political expertise via a speculative account of how it may be supposed to have developed in man. The essential feature of this reconstruction is that people, living naturally in small scattered groups, probably corresponding to families, are driven by necessity to form larger communities, but find that hostility between different groups makes communal life impossible. What is lacking is a sense of social solidarity transcending the natural kinship group, which would enable every individual to see every other as possessing rights not by virtue of a natural bond of kinship, but merely as a member of the community, and which would in consequence generate habits of self-restraint and respect for others. That is to say, they lacked *dikē* and *aidōs* (or their prosaic equivalents *dikaiosunē* and *sōphrosunē*). Moreover, these dispositions must not be the preserve of a special élite, but must be shared by all, for anyone lacking in them is potentially disruptive of the community. Gradually, the story tells us, by a long process of trial and error, this universal habit of mind was built up, finally allowing organized communities to develop.

Protagoras nowhere explains why one has to have special expertise to be entitled to speak on technical matters, but nothing beyond mere adulthood and rationality to speak on matters of public policy. He probably assumes that, while a technical expert is one who knows how best to attain an agreed end, questions of policy are themselves largely questions about what ends are to be pursued, and further that these questions are not susceptible of right and wrong answers, and hence there can be no one who is especially qualified to answer them. Rather, individuals have to make up their mind how they want to live and what sort of community they want to live in.

That doctrine would follow naturally from the more general subjectivist thesis which Protagoras maintained. Since he held that in general what each person believes is true for him or her, which I take to imply that the notion of impersonal truth, according to which a belief is true or false *simpliciter*, is an empty one, it will follow that what each person believes on matters of public policy is true for him or her, and that no view can be said to be just true or false. Since no opinion on how to conduct affairs is truer than any other, no one can claim any special authority for his or her opinion. But the *polis* must act in some way or other. Hence the most sensible rule is to let all opinions be heard and to act on the one which wins the most general assent. Hence Protagorean subjectivism might quite naturally (though not, of course, necessarily) lead to support for democracy.

321e *Art which Athena possesses*: Athena was associated with spinning and weaving, with pottery, and with the cultivation of the olive. The reference may be to any of these crafts.

322a *get food from the earth*: the reference is certainly to hunting and gathering, and perhaps also to agriculture.

323a *there can be no city at all*: Protagoras' position here (repeated at 324d–325a and at 326e–327a) is prima facie inconsistent with his commonsense admission (329e, 349d) that not every member of a civilized community is a good man. He would presumably reply that men who are unjust etc. by conventional standards are none the less good in the minimal sense required for participation in social life (327c–e). But while that defence removes the inconsistency, it prevents Protagoras from meeting Socrates' objection to his claim to teach excellence in the accepted sense.

2. THE JUDGEMENT OF SOULS (*Gorgias* 523a–527a)

ROBIN WATERFIELD

523a *the truth*: the 'myth' that follows may be compared with Plato's other eschatological myths at the end of *Phaedo* and *Republic* (and see also *Phaedrus* 246a ff.). As usual, Plato interweaves his own invention with folk tradition and mystical elements drawn from Pythagoreanism and Orphism. On these myths, see J. Annas, 'Plato's Myths of Judgement', *Phronesis*, 27 (1982), 119–43.

523a *between themselves*: Homer, *Iliad* 15. 187–93.

523b *Tartarus*: this was traditionally the lowest and most hellish part of the underworld, reserved for special criminals. The Isles of the Blessed were naturally described differently according to the predilections of the describer.

524a *Tartarus respectively*: the meadow first appears as the asphodel meadow of Homer's *Odyssey* 11. 539, and became a regular feature of the geography of the underworld. Some kind of crossroads is also a standard feature, at any rate where afterlife judgement is involved, because it is of course a topographical representation of judgement. See especially *Republic* 614c.

524a *from Europe*: it was commonly believed among the Greeks that there were only these two continents. They knew the northern African coast, but included it in one or the other of the two continents.

525b *to improve*: in the underworld, the dead can see other souls being punished, and this will help them to improve when they come to be reincarnated. Plato does not here express the doctrine of reincarnation which features in later dialogues, but his theory only makes sense in the context of such a doctrine. The idea that some people are incurably bad, and are punished only to deter others from committing crimes, sits awkwardly with the insistence at 472e and elsewhere that punishment is always good for the criminal. Perhaps Plato assumes that we can only count someone as incurable after his death.

525d *what Polus says is true*: 470d: 'Well, I don't need ancient history to help me prove you wrong, Socrates: there's enough counter-evidence from the very recent past for me to show that happiness and wrongdoing do commonly go together.'

525d *Homer testifies to this*: *Odyssey* 11. 572–600.

526b *token*: similar tokens appear at *Republic* 614c.

526c *Callicles*: Callicles declared his contempt for philosophy at 484c: 'The point is, Socrates, it's fine for a person to dabble in philosophy when he's the right age for it, but it ruins him if he devotes too much of his life to it.'

526c *same procedure*: that is, with those from Europe (523e–524a).

526c *among the dead*: *Odyssey* 11. 569.

526e *in this world*: there are plenty of echoes in Socrates' words here of
Callicles at 486a–c: 'And yet, my dear Socrates—now, please don't get
cross: it's because I'm fond of you that I'm going to say this—isn't this
state an embarrassment for you and anyone else who keeps going deeper
and deeper into philosophy? The point is that if you or any of your sort
were seized and taken away to prison, unjustly accused of some crime,
you'd be incapable—as I'm sure you're well aware—of doing anything
for yourself. With your head spinning and mouth gaping open, you
wouldn't know what to say. And if, when you appeared in court, you
were faced with a corrupt and unprincipled prosecutor, you'd end up
dead, if it was the death penalty he wanted. Oh, Socrates, "What a
clever discovery this is! It enables you to take a naturally gifted person
and ruin him." It makes a person incapable of defending himself or
of rescuing himself or anyone else from terrible danger; the best he can
hope for is that his enemies will steal all his property and let him live
on in his community with no status whatsoever, which would make his
situation such that anyone could smash him in the face (if you'll pardon
the extravagant expression) and not be punished for it.'

3. THE ANDROGYNE (*Symposium* 189c–193e)
ROBIN WATERFIELD

189d *happened to it*: despite Aristophanes' fame as a comic poet, the fantasy
that follows is Aesopic, aetiological folklore rather than learned comedy.
The analysis by Dover (1966) of the antecedents of and echoes in
Aristophanes' speech could hardly be bettered.

189e *as an insult*: it meant a coward, someone lacking in full manliness.

189e *forming a circle*: I follow the punctuation and interpretation of
J. S. Morrison, 'Four Notes on Plato's *Symposium*', *Classical Quarterly*,
14 (1964), 42–55. The fifth-century philosopher Empedocles had also
spoken of a former race of quasi-humans 'with faces and chests on
both sides' (fragment 61 Diels–Kranz), but there is little resemblance
to Aristophanes' theory, since for Empedocles these people were
grotesque, not perfect: they were of the same species as creatures who
were half-human, half-animal. Again, in fragment 62 Empedocles
spoke of a former race of 'whole-natured beings', but they seem to be
completely round, whereas Aristophanes' proto-humans have limbs.

190c *really about them*: see Homer, *Odyssey* 11. 307–20 (and the Index of
Names under Ephialtes). In Homer's account, Ephialtes and Otus were
huge giants, so Plato is having Aristophanes reinterpret Homer's story.

190e *with a hair*: it is possible to cut a hard-boiled egg in half with even a human hair. The point of the comparison is that the matter was easy for Zeus: it takes no more than a hair to cut an egg, and it took Zeus hardly any effort to cut our ancestors in half.

191b *or of a male whole*: it would be pedantic to point out that Aristophanes has missed out surviving halves of androgynous wholes: we get the point.

191c *like cicadas*: it is not quite clear what Plato thinks cicadas get up to, but in any case he is wrong: they have perfectly normal sex.

191d *our counterparts*: turbots and other flat-fish, Plato suggests, look like rounded fish which have been sliced in half. A 'tally' (*sumbolon*) was half an item given by a host to a departing guest; the host retained the other half, to show that the guest would always be recognized and welcome back in his house.

191e *adulteresses*: since marriages were mostly arranged, rather than being love-matches, a sexually consummated love-affair would tend to involve adultery.

191e *from this group*: this is the only extant reference in classical Greek literature to female homosexuality.

192a *in government*: both politics and homosexuality were largely upper-class concerns. This aside rather awkwardly interrupts the sequence of thought (halves of all-male originals when they are boys . . . and when they are men . . .). Plato undoubtedly included it for the echo of the comic motif (e.g. Aristophanes' own *Clouds* 1088 ff.) of accusing public figures of homosexuality. Aristophanes' theorizing may also contain a caricature of medical views such as those in the Hippocratic treatise *On Regimen I*, 27 ff., where the virility of manly men is explained by their having gained a greater quantity of male parts from *both* their parents (and *mutatis mutandis* the femininity of feminine women is explained in the same way).

193a *pursuit of wholeness*: it adds to the sadness of Aristophanes' doctrine of unfulfilled and unfulfillable longing that he is the only one of the named protagonists of the dialogue who is alone. Phaedrus is with Eryximachus in some sense (176d, 177a ff., 223b, *Phaedrus* 268a), the affair between Pausanias and Agathon was notorious, and so in its own way was that between Socrates and Alcibiades.

193a *the Arcadians*: our knowledge of Arcadian history and the fluctuating relations between Arcadia and Sparta is so patchy that one hesitates to deny categorically that this could refer to some incident prior to the dramatic date of *Symposium* (416). Nevertheless, it remains the case that the most likely event took place in 385, when the Spartans razed the city of Mantinea in Arcadia and dispersed or 'scattered' the population. If this is the incident Plato is referring to, he is being anachronistic;

but anachronisms occur in nearly all his works. On the issue, see H. B. Mattingly, 'The Date of Plato's *Symposium*', *Phronesis*, 3 (1958), 31–9, and K. J. Dover, 'The Date of Plato's *Symposium*', *Phronesis*, 10 (1965), 2–20.

193a *half-dice*: dice were commonly used as tallies (see note on 191d).

4. THE BIRTH OF LOVE (*Symposium* 201d–212c)
ROBIN WATERFIELD

201d *for ten years*: the famous plague struck Athens in 430, so Plato is referring to an incident in 440 (the plague is described by the historian Thucydides (2. 47–54), but identification of the infection is uncertain). We have no way of knowing whether or not Diotima was a real person or a fictional creation of Plato's, and we have no other evidence that there was fear of the plague as early as 440. It is safest to record an open verdict on the issue of Diotima's historicity and the truth of this incident. Mantinea was a real town, however, in eastern Arcadia; if Diotima is a fiction, a pun is certainly intended, since *mantis* means 'diviner', and the point of this anecdote is to introduce her as a wandering seer, of the kind states called on during war or other emergencies. The 'itinerant charismatic who provides cures for various needs' (W. Burkert, *Ancient Mystery Cults* (Cambridge, Mass.: Harvard University Press, 1987), 43) was a familiar figure in the ancient Greek world: the best known are Epimenides of Crete, Apollonius of Tyana, and St Paul. They served a number of purposes, but commonly offered initiations, so neither the form nor the content of Diotima's speech should come as a surprise.

202c *an enviable life*: all Greeks would have agreed that the gods have an enviable life, but their images of their gods were so thoroughly anthropomorphic that some gods *did* fall short of their notion of beauty (e.g. the crippled Hephaestus). But Diotima is a mouthpiece for Platonic ideas, and for Plato the concepts of badness and divinity were mutually exclusive.

203b *all the same*: Plotinus, the Neoplatonist of the third century AD, famously makes a great deal of Diotima's allegorical story in his essay on love (*Enneads* 3.5).

203d *no shoes on his feet*: especially since, by 204a, Love and philosophy become more or less identified, we are bound to be reminded of Socrates' habit of not wearing shoes (*Smp.* 174a), even in bitter cold (220b). Socrates is philosophy personified; later, in Alcibiades' speech, he becomes Love personified as well.

204a *isn't aware of lacking*: in Greek, 'love of knowledge' is *philosophia*. If Love falls between knowledge and ignorance, and is therefore philosophy, we begin to see that Socrates' claim to be an expert on Love (*Smp.* 177d, 198d) is not much different from his usual claim to know only that he is ignorant. Knowledge of ignorance is what impels a philosopher to try to gain knowledge, as Love does here. See also Plato's early dialogue *Lysis*, at 218b.

205a *seems conclusive*: because 'happiness' (*eudaimonia*) was for a Greek by definition the ultimate purpose of life. It is what fulfils you, whatever you take that to be.

205c *creators or poets*: Diotima's point in these two paragraphs is untranslatable in English. In Greek, the terms *poiēsis* and *poiētēs*, which basically just mean 'creativity' and 'creator', were usually reserved for 'poetry' and 'poet' (as in English 'artist' commonly means 'painter').

205d *dominant, deceitful love*: the words are probably a paraphrase from a verse of poetry.

205d *looking for their other halves*: this is, of course, an allusion to Aristophanes' speech, although Plato has Diotima speak in a vague way which allows him to maintain the fiction that Diotima is talking to Socrates long before the date of the (also fictional) symposium.

206b *may be called love*: so now Diotima reverts to discussing the specific kind of love which we commonly call 'love', rather than the generic kind she has outlined. Even the specific kind must be love of goodness, of course, but this will manifest in a specific fashion.

206b *in an attractive medium*: the Greek is literally 'procreation in something attractive'. The word 'in' should be taken at face value: the typical Greek attitude towards the female role in childbirth was that she was just a receptacle for the growth of the embryo, while all the properties of the child came from the father.

206c *a kind of birth*: Plato wants to link the concepts of immortality and the attractiveness of beauty. In this paragraph, he achieves this by conflating human male–female sexual intercourse with childbirth. We need to be attracted to someone to have sex with him or her; the purpose of sexual intercourse is childbirth; childbirth is the closest we get to attaining immortality. The conflation is particularly striking later in the paragraph (206d–e), where Plato comes up with a single set of images to cover aspects of both sex and birth. For instance, the talk of relaxation is meant to encompass both the reaction of the female genitalia to sexual excitement and the dilation of the cervix at birth (and vice versa for the talk of contraction); the talk of swelling is meant to remind us not only of a heavily pregnant woman, but also of an erect penis. The conflation of sex and childbirth is further complicated by an additional conflation of gender: since procreation was commonly seen as a specifically female function in ancient Greece, Diotima is turning these male lovers into women. For discussion of the passage and further references, see E. E. Pender, 'Spiritual Pregnancy in Plato's *Symposium*', *Classical Quarterly*, 42 (1992), 72–86.

206d *at childbirth*: this is just to say that beauty is responsible for childbirth.

206e *in a beautiful medium*: nevertheless, a great deal of emphasis continues to be placed on beauty as the object of love (especially at 210a–212a). But Diotima is not contradicting herself: she is driving a wedge between love's immediate, conscious object (which is beauty), and its long-term, subconscious object (which is procreation in a beautiful medium, as a means to happiness or possession of the good). The important distinction between conscious and subconscious desires first occurred in Aristophanes' speech (192c ff.).

207a *immortality as well*: it would be more natural to take the 'permanent' possession of goodness to mean possession throughout one's lifetime, and that is surely how the reader has been taking it since its introduction in 205a. We can forgive the fallacy, because of the importance of the insight that if our desires are limited to our own personal lifetimes, they take on a degree of futility. Once Diotima has understood 'permanence' as 'eternity', it is easy for her to unpack the desire as an implicit desire for immortality too. The introduction of eternity is helped not just by the general anticipatory nature of desire, but by the fact that Love has been shown to strive for things he does not have, and he was said at 202d to lack immortality.

208b *a body or whatever*: there is nothing here or in the previous paragraph which should lead us to think that at the time of writing *Symposium* Plato doubted the immortality of the human soul, or some part of it. This is a constant doctrine in other dialogues. In the previous paragraph, he is talking about low-level activities of the mind, which are particular to a given incarnation and therefore do not survive death; and in this paragraph he restricts himself to material objects, which are obviously perishable. To put this another way, in *Symposium* Plato is talking about the (necessarily limited) extent to which a specific person can be immortal, whereas in other dialogues he is talking about the immortality of souls (*psukhai*) which can, through reincarnation, be constituents of more than one person. Pythagoras may have been Euphorbus reincarnated, as he claimed, but that did not make him an identical person to Euphorbus.

208c *like a true sophist*: even though 'sophist' is invariably a term of insult in Plato, this phrase should not lead us to think that Plato doubted the value of Diotima's teaching. It is just that the sophists were notoriously—and often groundlessly—confident in the answers they gave. Some of them even made a display of inviting questions on *any* topic. So Diotima resembles a sophist only in being confident.

208c *fame immortal for ever*: the source of the line is unknown.

208d *joined Patroclus in death*: these were the two cases Phaedrus had made use of in his speech (179b–180b).

209c *education*: the emphasis here and in 210a–c on the educational aspect of a love-affair is supposed to remind us of Socrates' own conversations with young men, as immortalized in Plato's dialogues. The imagery of birth is bound to remind one of the famous metaphor of Socrates as a midwife of ideas in *Theaetetus* 148e–151d. The similarities and differences between the two passages are well discussed by M. F. Burnyeat, 'Socratic Midwifery, Platonic Inspiration', *Bulletin of the Institute of Classical Studies*, 24 (1977), 7–16, a paper which is reprinted in H. H. Benson, ed., *Essays on the Philosophy of Socrates* (Oxford: Oxford University Press, 1992), 53–65.

209c *ordinary children*: here children are seen as the glue of a relationship, in such a way that the warmth and permanence of an affair may be measured by the degree of affection felt for the children. Since the offspring of the kind of relationship Plato is talking about are more attractive and more immortal, and since we feel love for that which is attractive and immortal, then we are bound to feel more love for such offspring, and therefore there will be more warmth and permanence in this kind of relationship. It is relevant to remember the Athenian social context, that a man would not necessarily be expected to love his wife (the marriage would probably have been arranged), and yet she would be the one to bear his children: in such a situation, the bond of shared affection for children takes on great importance.

210a *Watcher*: this was an advanced grade of initiation in both the Eleusinian and the Samothracian mysteries. However, in the case of both these mystery cults, the secret has been well kept, and we do not know quite what the Watchers saw or did. The most accessible recent discussion of the Greek mysteries in general can be found in W. Burkert, *Ancient Mystery Cults* (note on 201d).

210a *his guide*: in the Eleusinian mysteries, the initiate would have been led by a guide—probably one of the officers known as Heralds—at certain stages. Outside the metaphor, the guide is perhaps Love (who makes a suitable herald, because he conveys messages etc. (202e–203a)), or perhaps the older partner in a relationship.

210e *proper order and manner*: a central part of the Eleusinian mysteries was the unveiling of certain ritually significant objects before the celebrant's eyes.

211b *entirely unaffected*: in expressing his conception of unchanging beauty, Plato not unnaturally drew on the vocabulary of the Presocratic philosopher-poet Parmenides, who claimed that in reality all is one and unchanging. See F. Solmsen, 'Parmenides and the Description of

Perfect Beauty in Plato's *Symposium*', *American Journal of Philology*, 92 (1971), 62–70.

211b *love for a boy*: we are reminded that male homoerotic love and 'mental' pregnancy have been the context all along. It is of course somewhat odd for Diotima—a woman—to be the expert in the higher mysteries of male homoerotic love. For an interesting discussion of this, and of other aspects of the dialogue which are concerned with sex and sexuality and reflect or reverse prevailing Athenian notions, see D. M. Halperin, 'Why is Diotima a Woman? Platonic Eros and the Figuration of Gender', in D. M. Halperin *et al.*, eds., *Before Sexuality: The Construction of Erotic Experience in the Ancient Greek World* (Princeton: Princeton University Press, 1990), 257–308. Basically, he concludes, Diotima is a woman (or rather—since she is plainly a Socratic *alter ego*—Socrates has to take on a female role) because women were considered the experts on reciprocity and on procreation.

211c *intellectual endeavour:* there are irresistible echoes in this paragraph of the upward ascent outlined in *Republic* 511b–c, which culminates in the vision of goodness, which is also called (e.g. at *R.* 504d) the ultimate intellectual endeavour.

212a *potential for immortality*: the only part of the mind which is immortal in itself is the intellect; the only mind or soul which is immortal as a whole is that which is wholly subservient to or one with the intellectual part. Again (see note on 208b) this is perfectly consistent with the doctrine of other dialogues.

5. THE OTHER WORLD (*Phaedo* 107c–115a)

DAVID GALLOP

107e *Aeschylus' Telephus*: an allusion to a lost play.

108a *the rites and observances followed here*: probably sacrifices made where three roads meet. Such practices belonged to the cult of Hecate, a goddess of the underworld, who was associated with magic and was worshipped at crossroads.

108d *the skill of Glaucus*: a proverbial expression, of uncertain origin, for the skill demanded by a difficult task.

109b *the Phasis River and the Pillars of Heracles*: the Phasis, which flowed into the eastern shore of the Black Sea, and the Pillars of Heracles (Gibraltar) lay at the eastern and western boundaries of the world inhabited by the Greeks.

109c *'ether'*: i.e. the sky, thought of as consisting of blue fire. The element is described in *Timaeus* (58d) as a rarefied form of air. The physical elements of our world are mere residues or 'dregs' from the pure and beautiful constituents of the 'true earth' that Socrates is about to describe. By representing the world familiar to us as a poor by-product of the 'real' world, his geological theory serves to illustrate a major theme of *Phaedo*; but it also shows Plato's eye for the wondrous beauty of the physical world itself.

110b *those twelve-piece leather balls*: play-balls made from twelve pieces of pliable leather, each in the shape of a regular pentagon, and sewn together to form a dodecahedron. This, when stuffed, would acquire the shape of a sphere.

112a *A great way off . . . beneath earth*: Iliad 8. 14.

6. THE CAVE (*Republic* 514a–517a)
ROBIN WATERFIELD

515a *no different from us*: this statement is unequivocal evidence that 'The Cave' is an *allegory*. The prisoners are said to be like us, but we do not spend our lives literally gazing at shadows of artefacts.

515c *inanity*: the kind of reorientation Plato envisages here is later typified, in an educational curriculum, by the effect of the mathematical sciences (521d ff.). But we need not suppose that mathematics is the *only* thing which can reorient one to break out of the shackles.

516b *in its proper place*: the sun in the allegory is, of course, goodness.

516d *without property*: Odyssey 11. 489.

517a *and kill him*: as Socrates was killed.

7. ER'S JOURNEY INTO THE OTHER WORLD (*Republic* 614b–621d)
ROBIN WATERFIELD

614b *Alcinous had to endure*: Odysseus' account of his adventures, told to Alcinous, occupies all of books 9–12 of Homer's *Odyssey*. There is a slight but untranslatable pun in the Greek: Er is described as *alkimos* ('brave')—a poetic word chosen for its cognate similarity to Alcinous' name; 'endure . . . endurance' at least goes some way towards capturing the light tone. As a piece of moral literature, the myth that now follows should just be read and enjoyed; the best critical and philosophical account is that of J. Annas, 'Plato's Myths of Judgement', *Phronesis*, 27 (1982), 119–43.

614c *judges*: traditional figures of an indeterminate number, but three became prominent—Minos, Rhadamanthys, and Aeacus. Belief in afterlife judgement (and therefore in some kind of crossroads in the underworld) was widespread in Greece.

614e *meadow*: the asphodel meadow of Homer's *Odyssey* 11. 539, which entered tradition as part of the geography of the underworld.

615a *a thousand years*: note how Plato plays with multiples of the Pythagorean sacred number ten throughout the myth; there are other Pythagorean and Orphic features in the myth, interwoven with tradition and Plato's invention. Plato's eschatological myths at the ends of *Gorgias* and of *Phaedo* are also well worth reading for comparison. The souls' time in the underworld is described as a journey because specific punishments for specific crimes were located in different regions of the underworld, so the souls would have gone from region to region before being allowed back.

615b *than the crime*: in other words, in the afterlife you relive your life ten times.

615c *isn't worth mentioning*: possibly they entered a kind of limbo, as Virgil records (*Aeneid* 6. 426–9): this is irrelevant to Plato's present purposes, for which he must stress rewards and punishments. This is his reason for not discussing their fate: I very much doubt that he is motivated by guilt (as some commentators have suggested) over his ambiguous suggestions about exposing unwanted children (460c, 461c).

616a *Tartarus*: the lowest and ghastliest region of Hades.

616c *the whole rotation together*: we know that Er is on the surface of the earth (614c ff.)—it may, however, be the 'real earth' of which the concluding myth of *Phaedo* speaks, in so far as it is not our familiar earth. He is taken on a journey to the centre of the universe; in Plato's geocentric view, this coincides with the centre of the earth. He approaches the shaft of light—soon to be called the spindle of Necessity too—which forms the central axis of the universe. Looking up, he can see that the ends of the outer rim of the universe join on to the shaft of light and stretch away from it:

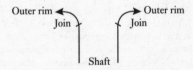

Notice how the shape resembles the top of a pillar, to which Plato has just likened the shaft. The shaft extends into a kind of strap which pulls the two halves of the universe together, and so the shaft maintains the integrity of the universe. (The naval simile refers, I think, to the cables which ran under a trireme, from one side to the other, ending in a tightening apparatus, and thus helped to keep the planks of wood together.)

616e *of the eighth whorl*: here is an ancient Greek spindle:

133

The spindle hung freely. The wool, drawn from the distaff, passed under
the hook (to keep the spindle upright) and was wound round the stem.
The whorl helped rotation and balance.

616e *of the second whorl*: the concentric whorls, viewed from above, would
have looked something like this:

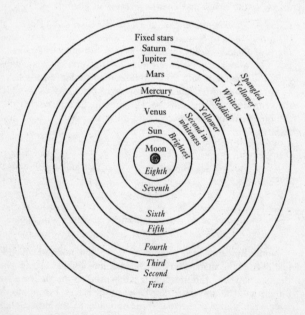

(Note that Plato here transposes Venus and Mercury.) Why do the
'rims' vary in broadness? And why in this way? It is difficult to say that
the differing widths represent Plato's views on the distances between the

planets, since at *Timaeus* 36d we meet an entirely different system for the distances between planets, and our passage seems to concern size rather than distance: distance is not really taken into account, since all the whorls fit 'snugly' inside one another.

In the *Timaeus* passage, as well as here, Plato is undoubtedly imagining the planets as being related to one another in terms of precise and meaningful mathematical ratios. In short, he is not trying to explain actual astronomical phenomena; he is concerned with arithmological theories like the Pythagorean Harmony of the Spheres (617b).

Although Plato chose not to assign actual values to the various widths in our passage (since his purpose is to impress the orderliness of the universe on our minds without boring us with minutiae), it is impossible to escape the impression that he did have particular values in mind. Given Plato's silence, informed guesswork is the best one can do; but it is worth noting, as justification for the attempt, that the assignment of different widths is certainly not as random as it may appear (see J. Cook Wilson, 'Plato, *Republic* 616e', *Classical Review*, 16 (1902), 292–3). Ordering the planets alphabetically from the outside of the whorl, and then assigning each of them a number according to the order of rim-size, we get clusters of additions up to 9:

It is clear that the context is musical; so it makes sense to look for some musically meaningful relationship between the rim-sizes. Although different ancient authors elaborated the Harmony of the Spheres by reference to different numbers of heavenly bodies, Plato shares with the scholar Eratosthenes (third century BC) the employment of eight bodies. There is a bizarre fragment of Eratosthenes (see Robin Waterfield, *The Theology of Arithmetic* (Grand Rapids, Mich.: Phanes Press, 1988), 104) which preserves a Pythagorean assignation of various values to the eight bodies, in such a way as to ensure that musical ratios occur time and again—the most important such ratios being the octave (2:1), the fourth (4:3), the fifth (3:2), and the tone (9:8). Here is a table showing Eratosthenes' assignations, and then ordering the same numbers according to Plato's ordering of the rim-sizes:

	Fixed Stars	♄	♃	♂	☿	♀	☉	☽
	A	B	C	D	E	F	G	H
Eratosthenes	36	32	24	21	12	16	18	9
Plato?	36	9	12	24	16	32	18	21

It would be more than foolish to claim that these values are at all certain, since Plato leaves no clues. However, this is the *kind* of thing he was up to. And note, in passing, that on this system the Harmony of the Spheres is a triple octave (36:9).

617a *not as white as the third*: these colours are clearly assigned on the basis of observation, plus the theoretical knowledge—gained originally from the Presocratic philosopher Parmenides of Elea (fl. *c.*475), as far as we know—that the moon reflects the sun's light.

617a *the direction of the whole*: from a geocentric point of view, the planets appear to travel from west to east, while the diurnal movement of the whole heaven is from east to west.

617b *and fifth*: from the geocentric point of view, the sun, Venus, and Mercury all take about a year to circle the earth; the moon takes some 29.5 days; Mars takes 687 days; Jupiter takes about twelve years; Saturn takes about 29.5 years.

617b *retrograde motion*: of course, all the planets periodically appear retrograde from a geocentric perspective; Plato's mention of the phenomenon in the case of Mars is a mere embellishment of his narrative.

617d *condemned to impermanence*: this must refer to the impermanence of repeated incarnations, since the souls themselves are immortal.

617e *your own deities*: that is, the *genius* or guardian spirit of your life—which, ultimately, makes you the particular individual you are, with your predilections and life-pattern. It steered you, in Greek thought, subconsciously (see 620e); but a particularly advanced individual such as Socrates could consciously hear its voice.

618c *at any given moment*: so our prenatal choice of life does not determine our destiny once and for all time. We can reinforce or change that choice at every instant of our lives (within a predetermined framework: see note on 620e). This elusive sentence invites us to read the myth as not only concerned with a time between incarnations, but also as allegorical for a 'time' when one is in an altered state of consciousness within one's own lifetime: famous examples of such revelatory mystical visions include those of Muhammad and St Teresa of Avila.

619b *stupidity and greed*: it is odd to find the soul, which has just been said to be tripartite only because of its involvement with the physical world (611b–612a), liable after death to the kind of base motives we have come to associate with the lower parts of the mind/soul. It may be that even after a thousand years of purgation traces remain of one's previous incarnation: this is the implication of 619c–d.

619c *eating his own children*: as legendary dictators such as Thyestes had done.

620a *amusing, and astonishing*: in other words, it aroused precisely the emotions Plato expressed disapproval of earlier in *Republic*. It is arguable that the myth is meant to be an example of the kind of story-telling Plato finds acceptable. It is in prose, and it tells a moral tale. Another clue to the same reading of the myth lies in the predominance of the heroes of the Homeric poems and fifth-century tragedies.

620a   *a female incarnation*: the Greeks regarded all swans as male. Swans were famous for their 'swansong' at the approach of death; hence Plato will shortly classify them as songbirds, and it makes a suitable incarnation for the musician Orpheus, as (more obviously) the nightingale does for Thamyras.

620b   *about the armour*: after Achilles' death, Ajax laid claim to his armour—symbolically to his status as supreme Greek champion. To Ajax's chagrin, however, it was awarded to Odysseus: in consequence, Ajax killed himself. Nevertheless, Ajax's prowess matches that of a lion, as Agamemnon's nobility does that of an eagle.

620e   *unalterable*: perhaps we are to imagine one of them spinning the warp, and the other the woof, of a person's life. There are clear astrological connotations to the passage: the word translated 'destiny' also means (or came to mean) 'degree on the zodiacal circle'; 'ratify' is cognate with the rulership of a planet. In short, as well as setting an individual's destiny in a more abstract sense, the Fates do so according to the positions of the planets (Atropos) and the zodiacal signs (Clotho). Note that, despite Plato's use of the word 'unalterable' (and see also 618b on temperament), it is only the broad framework which is fixed; the whole of Plato's philosophy leaves room for self-improvement within that framework. Annas, 'Plato's Myths of Judgement' (note on 614b), overstresses the predetermination and downplays the element of moment-by-moment choice. She also finds the myth incompatible with the rest of the book in that it portrays a universe in which there is an overall balance of good and bad, such that one individual's personal contribution cannot make any difference. And in other dialogues Plato holds out the prospect of breaking free of the cycles of incarnation, as a result of unmitigated goodness; the myth of *Republic* is surprisingly silent on this score, but it is not incompatible with his vision here.

621a   *the Plain of Oblivion*: a familiar geographical feature of the underworld in Greek thought, as is a variously named river to make one forget. The lack of shelter from the heat appears to be a Platonic invention—perhaps to explain the souls' instinctive willingness to drink from the river.

621a   *the required amount*: presumably those who drink less can be more conscious in their next incarnation: they stand a better chance of recollection, perhaps. Plato does call philosophers awake or conscious elsewhere. It is odd that we are supposed to choose a life and *then* forget; but it is a common religious notion that each of us is here on earth for some particular purpose which is preordained in some way and which we have to work to uncover.

621b *shooting stars*: there is a not uncommon belief that on death people's souls become stars. Plato probably got the idea from the Middle East.

621b *funeral pyre*: see 614b.

621b *to the end*: a traditional phrase for ending a story.

621d *of our story*: see 615a.

8. THE WINGED SOUL (*Phaedrus* 246a–257a)
ROBIN WATERFIELD

246a *his team of horses*: the doctrine of the tripartite soul is argued for most famously and fully at *Republic* 434d–441c. It is given a physiological basis at *Timaeus* 69c ff. But even so Plato can talk in a more accessible fashion, using a simple dichotomy between the rational and irrational parts of the soul. It is just that, in fact, the irrational parts are two.

246a *are a mixture*: it is significant that even the gods' souls are tripartite. There is continuity between human and divine souls: they both have the same impulse, to see the Forms. But there are also differences: the gods are untroubled by conflict, and are therefore never incarnated into a physical body. The presence of both horses in the human soul shows that, contrary to many conceptions of the soul in the history of Western thought, Plato does not regard the soul as basically either good or bad. It innately has both good impulses and bad impulses, and it depends on reason—the charioteer—which of the two wins out.

246b *is called 'mortal'*: a question that is made urgent by the doctrine that every living creature has an immortal soul, and is answered by a theory of reincarnation.

246b *all that is inanimate*: throughout his life Plato was convinced, sometimes in a markedly ascetic fashion, of the superiority of the soul to the body, and of mental or psychic goods to physical and external goods. So, for instance, in the early dialogues we are urged to take care of our souls to the virtual exclusion of all else. It is only in his latest dialogue, *Laws*, that Plato fully admits that souls can harm a body (896e), by the lifestyle they choose, for instance.

247a *eleven squadrons*: there were canonical lists of the twelve Olympian gods, but they differed slightly. Given Plato's separation here of Hestia, the goddess of the hearth (perhaps as an image of the earth at the centre of the heavens), he is probably thinking of Zeus, Hera, Hephaestus, Aphrodite, Ares, Poseidon, Demeter, Apollo, Artemis, Athena, Hermes, and Dionysus; these are precisely the twelve familiar to Athenians from the east frieze of the Parthenon. The 'spirits' Plato mentions are probably the various demigods assigned to these major deities (as Eros was Aphrodite's companion, and the Sea-nymphs were Poseidon's), but given what is said at 252c–d they may include the guardian spirits which look after a person in his lifetime and are said in *Republic* to represent the destiny of the incarnation a person has chosen (*Republic* 620d–621a). While the gods in *Phaedrus* appear to retain their traditional Greek roles, they are also astral deities, driving the stars and planets. There is a hint of astral spirits at *Republic* 621b and the gods reappear as astral deities at *Timaeus* 40a–b and *Laws* 966d–967d.

247a *each performing his proper function*: there is an echo of an important element of *Republic*. In *Republic* 'performing one's own function' is what unifies the ideal city and the human soul, for which the city is an analogy. The gods in *Phaedrus* perform their own function, and they are so unified that it is impossible to distinguish between driver and team of horses.

247b *we call 'immortal'*: strictly speaking, every soul is immortal, but in common parlance we think of only the gods as immortal. It is very unlikely that the spatial imagery in what follows is to be taken literally. This is a controversial aspect of Plato's metaphysics, but although he often speaks of two worlds, the intelligible world and the world of the senses, there is more overlap between them than many scholars have thought. Thus, for instance, in *Phaedrus* as elsewhere, it is the sight of beautiful things in this world that reminds us and sets us in search of absolute Beauty. The 'separation' of the Forms (see next note) is metaphysical difference, not physical separation: they are different in that they are not liable to change and decay, they are immaterial, and so on. But the fact that we do not perceive them is, at least in part, a fault of our perception, not just of their difference (see e.g. 250e).

247e *and returns home*: there can be little doubt that the entities the soul sees in the 'region beyond heaven' are the Forms (as they are usually called), though the religious awe with which they are invested in *Phaedrus* is striking: they alone are what is really real (247c, 249c); they are called 'sacred' (250a), and they occupy a 'holy' place (254b), which is higher even than the gods' home (247e); in fact, the divinity of the gods is somehow due to the Forms (249c), and the gods' minds are fed by the sight of the Forms (247d). This passion alone makes it hard to believe the view of Nehamas (in A. Nehamas and P. Woodruff, *Plato:* Phaedrus (Indianapolis: Hackett, 1995)) that Plato is using the palinode to bid farewell to his middle-period views on Forms.

Here Plato mentions 'justice as it really is', self-control, and knowledge, and describes the domain as a whole as 'true being'. Such a description is standard for the Forms, as is the suffix 'as it really is'; also, the Forms are always immaterial, immutable, and perfect. Though there is argument about the scope of the theory (are there Forms of everything in the world, even beds and chairs, or only of disputable predicates such as beauty?), justice and beauty (250b) are Forms that appear elsewhere in the dialogues, and self-control and knowledge (that is, knowledge of Forms) are comprehensible Forms too, given that here, in typical middle-period mode, Plato is stressing the perfection of Forms, as standards of which their counterparts on earth will inevitably fall short. However, the assumption here that there is a kind of perfect knowledge correlated only with Forms is used at *Parmenides* 133b–134e as the basis of an argument designed to prove that we mortal humans *cannot* have such knowledge. In different contexts in the dialogues, Plato urges us to think of Forms either as perfect standards with pale imitations in the material world, or as entities in which the things of this world partake and which they are named after. The best accounts of Plato's 'theory' of Forms are: A. Wedberg, *Plato's Philosophy of Mathematics* (Stockholm: Almquist & Wiksell, 1955), 26–44; and J. Annas, *An Introduction to Plato's* Republic (Oxford: Oxford University Press, 1981), 190–241. See also the essays collected in vol. i of G. Fine, ed., *Plato*, (2 vols. Oxford: Oxford University Press, 1999) and vol. ii of N. D. Smith, ed., *Plato: Critical Assessments* (4 vols. London: Routledge, 1998).

247e *to wash the ambrosia down*: Plato is alluding light-heartedly to Homer, *Iliad* 5. 368–9, where the goddess Iris reins in the team of horses she has been lent by Ares and throws them some ambrosia to eat. D. Blyth ('The Ever-Moving Soul in Plato's *Phaedrus*', *American Journal of Philology*, 118 (1997), 185–217, p. 190) may well be right to suggest that this feeding of the horses of the gods' souls is, as it were, the earthing of their souls, so that they have enough connection with physical existence to perform their function of taking care of the world. Note also that this food is the horses' equivalent of the food the gods themselves have been eating in the previous paragraph—the vision of the Forms. By implica-tion, our souls too are nourished by the sight of the Forms (see *Phaedo* 84a–b, *Republic* 490b). The Forms are not just abstract philosophical entities, but a source of life (as are impressions in general: *Republic* 401b–c). We are in the thick of the religious and mystical dimension of Plato's thought, which has been well summarized in the context of this dialogue by K. Seeskin, 'Plato, Mysticism and Madness', *Monist*, 59 (1976), 574–86.

248a *resemble him most*: on the Platonic ideal of 'assimilation to god', see especially *Theaetetus* 172c–177b and *Timaeus* 90b–d, with J. Annas, *Platonic Ethics Old and New* (Ithaca, NY: Cornell University Press, 1999), ch. 3, and D. Sedley, 'The Ideal of Godlikeness', in Fine, *Plato*, ii. 309–28 (see first n. to 247e).

248b *specious nourishment*: the word translated 'specious' is cognate with *doxa*, which is Plato's usual word for 'opinion', the mental faculty contrasted with knowledge.

248b *the plain of truth*: a Pythagorean called Petron of Himera also used this phrase (according to Plutarch, at any rate, in *On the Decline of Oracles* 422b–e), and he is usually thought to have lived before Plato, in which case this may be evidence of Plato's borrowing from Pythagorean tradition. But Petron's dating is uncertain, and Plutarch, as a Platonist, may have embellished his account with this phrase. There are also echoes in what follows of the Presocratic philosopher Empedocles, on which see R. Hackforth, *Plato's* Phaedrus (Cambridge: Cambridge University Press, 1952), 82.

248d *dedicated to love*: although the Greek reads, literally, 'philosophers or lovers of beauty or men of culture or men who are dedicated to love', it is clear that in no case is the 'or' meant to be disjunctive. A few lines later, at 249a, the same character will be glossed as 'a man who has practised philosophy with sincerity or combined his love for a boy with the practice of philosophy'. Or again, at *Phaedo* 61a Plato has Socrates say that 'the highest music is philosophy' ('men of culture' being literally 'men devoted to the Muses'), and the connection between philosophy (literally 'love of wisdom') and love of beauty is maintained throughout Diotima's speech in *Symposium*, which also shows, as *Phaedrus* does too, how important dedication to love is for a philosopher in the Platonic mould.

These philosophic souls must belong to the second of the three categories of soul described in the previous paragraph. The first category, those who catch a good, even if not quite perfect, glimpse of reality, are not liable to incarnation in this cycle, but the other two categories (those who, almost comically, bob up and down across the frontier of the plain of truth, and those who altogether fail to see reality) are to be incarnated. Incarnation is a result of ignorance (failure to see the truth), and anything less than complete knowledge of truth is enough to guarantee incarnation.

248d *initiators into one of the mystery cults*: given the mystical tone of this stretch of our dialogue, it may come as a surprise to see how low Plato ranks prophets and initiators. But as *Republic* 364e–365a shows, Plato did not think highly of most such people, who claimed to be able to provide instant fixes for past sins. Redemption, in Plato's view, is a long, hard process.

248e *tyrants*: in *Gorgias* and *Republic* too Plato ranks tyrants as the lowest form of human life. It is an implication of *Phaedrus* 248c and 249b that after one of these nine sorts of first incarnation, a failed soul would be born into the body of an animal; in *Timaeus*, a possible second incarnation, between becoming a man and becoming an animal, is becoming a woman. Plato's belief in reincarnation is most vividly expressed in the myth with which he ends *Republic*.

The ranking here in *Phaedrus* is mysterious, but probably depends on a number of factors: how much knowledge the pursuits involve; what kind of knowledge the pursuits involve; the social value of the pursuits; the political value of the pursuits (on Plato's understanding of political value as determined by ability to see to the true welfare of the citizens); and whether they care for the soul or the body. If I had to summarize all this simply, I would say that the ranking depends on how large the view of the world is for which the person acts as a channel, or in other words how much he is possessed, or in other words (perhaps) how transcendent is the object he loves, or in other words how much control he has over the black horse of his internal chariot, to aid his recollection of the vision of true Beauty he once had.

248e *the opposite*: does this refer to the punishment awaiting them in the underworld between incarnations, or to reincarnation at a different level among the nine ranks just listed? Comparison with *Laws* 903c–905c suggests the latter, though most scholars prefer the former.

248e *ten thousand years*: is the soul at this point necessarily perfect, free from internal conflict, and therefore free from further incarnation? Perhaps not: see R. S. Bluck, 'The *Phaedrus* and Reincarnation', *American Journal of Philology*, 79 (1958), 156–64. Bluck argues that the fall of souls who have failed to catch a glimpse of true reality in the plain of truth is not the original fall; they have been on earth before, and after ten thousand years they simply resume the struggle described at 248a–c to see the truth. But he is decisively refuted by D. D. McGibbon, 'The Fall of the Soul in Plato's *Phaedrus*', *Classical Quarterly*, 14 (1964), 56–63.

249a *they return*: at *Phaedo* 80d–81a, however, philosophers have to undergo only a single incarnation.

249b *in human form*: other myths of afterlife judgement can be found at the end of *Gorgias* and *Republic*. There Plato allows for the possibility that some souls are so wicked that they endure eternal punishment, whereas in *Phaedrus* all souls, however wicked, seem to regain their wings after ten thousand years, or ten incarnations.

249b *the life it likes*: The brevity of the statement here compared to the fullness of the version in *Republic* 617d–620d strongly suggests that *Phaedrus* was written after *Republic*.

249c *into true reality*: according to the 'theory of Recollection' recognition of attributes is recollection of pre-incarnate knowledge of Forms. The best recent discussion is D. Scott, *Recollection and Experience: Plato's Theory of Learning and its Successors* (Cambridge: Cambridge University Press, 1995); a more summary version of his views can be found in Fine, *Plato*, vol. 1 (see on 247e). Plato's argument here is a little obscure, but may be paraphrased as follows: if a soul did not already possess latent knowledge of the singular Forms, it is impossible to conceive how a man could make sense of the variety of sense impressions and group them under single abstract concepts. And so it is unthinkable that a soul could start its existence as an animal, because as an animal it could not have gained the knowledge that enables it to abstract from sense impressions in this way. And so it must have been out on the rim of the universe, and then have been born as a man, before degenerating into animalhood, and then returning to human form.

249d *behaving like a madman*: compare especially the apocryphal story about Thales, an archetypal philosopher, told by Plato at *Theaetetus* 174a–b. Every human soul desires to know Forms, and has an ability to do so. But both the desire and the ability may be overridden by the black horse, unless it is restrained. The philosopher alone has the desire and the ability in full. 'The rapture that marks his success Plato calls "love", and the look of otherworldly devotion in his eyes others call "madness"' (M. L. Morgan, 'Philosophical Madness and Political Rhetoric in the *Phaedrus*', ch. 6 of his *Platonic Piety: Philosophy and Ritual in Fourth-century Athens* (New Haven: Yale University Press, 1990), 177). Plato here compresses the gradual ascent to the Form of Beauty as described in *Symposium* 210a–211c: the various stages of the ascent are implied simply by the assertion that the philosopher 'looks upward'.

249e *anyone who is touched by it*: i.e. especially the lover's beloved: see 255a–256b.

249e *this kind of madness*: Plato may be hazarding an etymology of *erastēs* (lover) from the Greek words for 'love' and 'best'.

250b *we as attendants of Zeus*: we have to wait till 252e to find out that followers of Zeus are philosophers, and so that this is what Plato means here by 'we'.

250c *imprisoned like shellfish*: the last four English sentences translate a single, passionately long sentence in the Greek, which is filled with the terminology of the Eleusinian Mysteries (for a brief account of which see W. Burkert, *Greek Religion* (Oxford: Basil Blackwell, 1985), 285–90). The word translated 'untainted by' could also mean 'unentombed in', and is a reference to the Orphic teaching which was neatly captured in Greek in the phrase *sōma sēma*: 'the body is a tomb.'

250c *rather too long now*: an unusual admission from Plato's Socrates that he is one of the initiates, a true philosopher. This is of more than passing interest in context, because at 246a Socrates said that he would produce at best only an image of what the soul is like, and at 273d he says that the best images or likenesses are produced by those who know the truth. As one who knows the truth, then, Socrates is inviting us to regard the myth of the soul as a good likeness.

250d *and especially lovable*: in other words, love of beauty (the experience which is being described as a means to philosophical contemplation) is as close as a human being can get to genuine philosophy (literally, 'love of wisdom'), which is presumably part of the god's divine experience.

251a *unnatural pleasures*: it has been said that this sentence contains a 'contemptuous reference to heterosexual love' and that 'Plato regarded this as deserving of equal condemnation with the unnatural pursuit of pleasure (i.e. a purely carnal homosexual relationship) of which he speaks in the same breath' (Hackforth, *Plato's* Phaedrus, 98 (see first n. to 248b). While it is true that in the second part of the sentence Plato seems to be condemning homosexual intercourse as unnatural, it is not clear that what he is condemning in the first part is heterosexual love in general, rather than the wasting of the energy which is love on the lesser goal of procreation as opposed to the more important goal of attaining immortality (see *Symposium* 208e ff.).

251a *a cult statue or a god*: this seems to be a Greek idiom for being thunderstruck by love: Plato uses it again at *Charmides* 154c. But here in *Phaedrus* the expression gains further overtones, because we know that lover and beloved are followers of the same god. Thus the beloved adumbrates his god just as his beauty adumbrates Beauty. Once the lover has overcome his confusion and lust (253c–255a), the lover sees the beloved as 'godlike' (255a) and the beloved sees that the lover is 'inspired by a god' (255b).

251c *we call it desire*: Plato is hazarding an extremely fanciful etymology, according to which *himeros* ('desire') is derived from the *i* in the Greek word for 'approach', *merē* ('particles'), and *rhein* ('flow').

252b *call him 'Pteros'*: the lines are presumably a Platonic invention, so that half the joke is attributing them to an august figure such as Homer. 'Pteros' is a made-up word, derived from the words for 'winged' and 'love'. They may also be the hint of an obscenity, since *anapterō* (literally 'to flap the wings') can mean 'to excite sexually' (as it does at the end of 255c). The metrical irregularity is that in the first half of the second line a short syllable is treated as short before the consonants *pt*, while in the second half another short syllable is lengthened before the same consonants.

253a *gazing on the god*: two processes are going on at once: the discovery or rediscovery by lovers of their own proper god, and the development of their beloved's discovery or rediscovery. In the case of followers of Zeus, the philosopher's god, this means that in helping others to become philosophers, one develops as a philosopher oneself. The lover's subconscious ('remembered') awareness of his natural god helps him to discover his soul-mate and to develop both his own and his lover's potential.

253a *Bacchant-like*: they are so happy to have found the potential image of their god on earth, in the boy they fall in love with, that they make him as close an image as they can. This not only makes the boy even more like their god, but also brings into consciousness their own awareness of which god they are the servants of. Both these things make them love the boy all the more, which makes them all the more want him to fulfil his Zeus-like potential . . . and so on in a never-ending spiral of increasing love. This behaviour is said to be 'Bacchant-like' because Bacchants infect others with their own enthusiasm for their god, Dionysus.

253b *the same qualities as themselves*: from which it follows that, contrary to hints dropped earlier in the dialogue (e.g. at 248d) and in *Symposium* that the only true lover is a philosopher, others (followers of gods other than Zeus) can also be lovers and therefore philosophers. Plato is clearly talking about twelve different types of human character, which are to be explained as dedication to a particular god. For more thoughts on the discrepancy between the idea that only followers of Zeus can be philosophers, and the idea that the followers of any god can be philosophers, see M. Dyson, 'Zeus and Philosophy in the Myth of Plato's *Phaedrus*', *Classical Quarterly*, 32 (1982), 307–11.

253b *dealings with their beloveds*: we already know from 247a that there is no 'meanness' (*phthonos*) among the gods, and from elsewhere in Socrates' palinode that the lover assimilates himself to his god. So there is no meanness in his attitude towards his boyfriend, and this is undoubtedly meant to contrast with the spiteful jealousy which characterized both Lysias' non-lover and the disguised lover of Socrates' first speech. See M. W. Dickie, 'The Place of *Phthonos* in the Argument of Plato's *Phaedrus*', in R. M. Rosen and J. Farrell, eds., *Nomodeiktes: Greek Studies in Honor of Martin Ostwald* (Ann Arbor: University of Michigan Press, 1993), 379–96.

253d *the better position*: in a chariot drawn by a pair of horses the more reliable horse was put on the right, the less reliable one on the left.

253d *only by spoken commands*: for a more detailed and less anthropomorphic description of the qualities of a good horse, by a contemporary of Plato, see Xenophon, *On Horsemanship* 1. Plato seems to assume that these horses are male, though in fact it was more usual to use mares for chariot teams. This is because his horses are thinly disguised humans.

254a *the pleasures of sex*: notice that the good horse is here assumed *always* to be an ally of the charioteer, our rational faculty. This effectively makes the soul bipartite rather than tripartite.

254b *next to self-control*: in the context of talk of memory, images of statues on pedestals are bound to remind one of a common memory technique, which precisely involves picturing qualities as statues, in order to fix them clearly in the memory where they can act as focal points around which to cluster further memories. In ancient and medieval times such memory systems were an important part of the orator's training, so that he could remember whole speeches or declaim on any subject about which he was asked. We know that the statue-imaging system was in use in Roman times, and we know that Socrates' contemporary Hippias of Elis had a memory system, though we do not know what kind it was. On the whole subject, see F. A. Yates, *The Art of Memory* (London: Routledge & Kegan Paul, 1966).

254e *in reverence and awe*: or, as we would say nowadays, his desire has been suppressed or sublimated. Desire has not been transformed, as some commentators think. It is not that the black horse is frightened of the boy, so that lust has been transformed to fear: it fears the punishment it would receive from the charioteer if it sprang lustfully on the boy.

255c *in love with Ganymede*: in de Vries's words (G. J. de Vries, *A Commentary on the* Phaedrus *of Plato* (Amsterdam: Hakkert, 1969), 174): 'The fantastic etymology of *himeros*, proposed in 251c, is here playfully sanctioned by attributing it to the god whom philosophers especially are said to follow.'

255d *cannot say where it came from*: it was an ancient Greek folk belief that it was possible to catch ophthalmia just from someone's glance, by a mysterious process similar to that by which a yawn is contagious.

256b *Olympic bouts*: at the Olympic games, a wrestler had to throw his opponent three times to win. Plato uses this as a metaphor for the three lifetimes of philosophy that are required to break out of the wheel of reincarnation (see 249a). The metaphor is suitable since the Olympic games were sacred to Zeus, and so are philosophers, according to Plato; but he insists that living three lives as a philosopher is even tougher than winning at the real Olympic games.

256c *prestige rather than philosophy*: in this paragraph Plato shows himself to be sympathetic to the second rank of person, the 'timocratic' man of *Republic* 9.

257a *nine thousand years*: see 248e–249b: 9,000 years is the total time between successive incarnations. What Plato means by a discarnate soul roaming around and under the earth is presumably what is hinted at in *Phaedo* 81c–e, that some souls are so laden with earthy elements that they have to stay near the earth, where they are occasionally visible as ghosts.

9. THE TWO COSMIC ERAS (*Statesman* 268d–274e)

ROBIN WATERFIELD

268e *what's supposed to have happened*: the story was familiar and Euripides had given it prominence in two of his surviving plays (*Orestes* 988–1009, *Electra* 699–746) and in at least one lost one. For killing Oenomaus (in order to win his daughter) and Myrtilus (who had helped him kill Oenomaus), Pelops' family was cursed by the gods. Right of kingship was to be decided between his two sons, Atreus and Thyestes, by possession of a golden-fleeced lamb. Thyestes gained the lamb by underhand means, but Zeus caused the heavenly bodies to change direction as a sign of his displeasure: Atreus, not Thyestes, was to have the throne. At *Histories* 2. 142 Herodotus says that the periodic reversal of the motion of the heavenly bodies was ancient Egyptian lore. Plato makes it clear that he is going to combine this traditional myth with two others—that there was a time, the age of Cronus, when people lived a life of leisure, and that in ancient times people were born directly from the earth.

269a *the god*: Zeus.

269e *partially material*: it soon becomes clear that the universe is like a human body writ large: it is animated matter, a combination of matter and soul, and has all the properties of a human soul, such as memory and desire.

269e *the initiator of all motion*: for discussion of Plato's thoughts on the initiator of motion, see T. M. Robinson, 'Demiurge and World Soul in Plato's *Politicus*', *American Journal of Philology*, 88 (1967), 57–66.

270a *a pair of gods with conflicting purposes*: however, elsewhere Plato speculates that there might be *two* sources of motion—one of good and one of evil. But there are so many difficulties and seeming inconsistencies in Plato's various accounts of the origin of evil (especially in *Timaeus* and *Laws*) that it seems best to read each passage on its own.

270a *its maker*: the word is the same as that used in *Timaeus* for the Demiurge or creator god.

270a *the tiny 'foot' it uses for travelling*: this is highly obscure, but seems to be a way of expressing the idea that little friction was involved. At any rate, the mechanistic explanation offered here for the reverse motion of the universe sits awkwardly with the talk at 272e of the universe somehow desiring its motion.

271b *for some other destiny*: perhaps freedom from further incarnations: see *Phaedrus* 249a.

271c *Cronus' regime*: the traditional Golden Age, set in the distant past. Work in Greece was largely agricultural and hard, and so a life of leisure was a feature of the Golden Age at least from Hesiod onwards (*Works and Days* 109–26, written about 700 BCE). Though in the original story leisure was enough to make everyone happy, Plato qualifies this: they were happy only if they used their minds appropriately as well.

272b *under Zeus*: perhaps the most puzzling feature of the myth is this: why is Zeus, a benign god, said to be in charge of the universe during its reverse rotation and descent into chaos? Related questions are: why does Plato sometimes talk in abstract terms of a period when the universe is under an unnamed god and a period when it is unwinding of its own accord, and sometimes in concrete terms of a period when the universe is under Cronus and one when it is under Zeus? And how can we reconcile the idea that the world gradually declines towards a chaotic *end* with the idea that there is cosmic catastrophe at the *start* of each cycle? Some scholars think that Plato has in mind a three-stage process: the rule of Cronus, a transitional period of catastrophe, and the rule of Zeus. But this is hard to square with the text, which seems to assume only two different cycles (with strong echoes of the Presocratic philosopher Empedocles). Perhaps both Cronus and Zeus are considered as tutelary deities, responsible for the human herd and subordinate to the unnamed god. And I suspect that the model Plato has in mind for the universe is a spindle, as in *Republic*'s 'Myth of Er'; it is then easy to see how after an initial period of tremors the spindle could spin smoothly before starting to run down into disorder.

274d *the goddess who shares his skill:* Athena.

274e *put it to work*: the helmsman/herdsman god of the myth has the three main talents of a good ruler: they both manage their wards in such a way as to maximize their happiness; they both try to save their wards from disorder and evil; and they both resolve opposition into harmony. Plato himself acknowledges later in the dialogue that the morals he wants to derive from the myth could have been stated more briefly, but he clearly enjoyed the story for itself, and (see M. S. Lane, *Method and Politics in Plato's 'Statesman'* (Cambridge: Cambridge University Press, 1998), 99–117) there are echoes within the myth of methodologies and themes from elsewhere in the dialogue.

10. ATLANTIS AND THE ANCIENT CITY OF ATHENS

ROBIN WATERFIELD

Timaeus 20d–25d

20e *the seven sages*: the seven sages were the traditional wise men of Greece, dating back to the Archaic period (800–500 BCE). At the beginning of the sixth century, Solon temporarily took control of Athens in order to revise the constitution and prevent civil war between the wealthy landowners and the peasants who worked for them. In Plato's time, orators were calling him the founder of Athenian democracy, though in fact the system he established was a meritocracy and, strictly speaking, democracy had to wait for Cleisthenes at the end of the sixth century. Plato remains the sole source of the Atlantis story told here, which is certainly a Platonic fiction.

20e *in his verses*: not in any of the surviving fragments, which focus almost exclusively on describing and justifying his political reforms. Plato has deliberately compressed Critias' family tree to reduce the likelihood that over the generations the story had become distorted. By the same token he will shortly try out the barefaced lie that Solon's poetry was 'new' when Critias was about 10 years old, over a hundred years after its composition.

20e *the destruction of human life*: Plato believed in the periodic destruction of human life by cosmic catastrophes: see *Statesman* 270c–d, *Critias* 111a–b, *Laws* 677a–678a.

21a *her festival*: Athena, the patron deity of Athens, was celebrated above all in an annual festival called the Panathenaea. The festival was, among many other things, an excuse for Athenians to recall the great exploits of the past, such as their defeat in 490 of the Persians at the battle of Marathon. For similarities between Critias' speech and the speeches typically given at the Panathenaea, see K. A. Morgan, 'Designer History: Plato's Atlantis Story and Fourth-Century Ideology', *Journal of Hellenic Studies*, 118 (1998), 101–18.

21b *the Koureotis of the Apatouria*: the Apatouria was a late-autumn festival on the third day of which each year's crop of male children were presented to their father's phratry. The day was named 'Koureotis' after the boys (*kouroi*).

21c *phratry*: literally, 'brotherhood'. Phratries, relics of archaic Athens, were kinship groupings of citizens with certain religious and social functions.

21c *more independent than anyone else*: because he was not paid to write his poems by a patron who expected some acknowledgement and flattery, but did so for his own purposes.

21e *King Amasis*: on Amasis (Aahmes), see Herodotus 2. 172 ff. with Lloyd's notes (Alan Lloyd, *Herodotus Book II* (3 vols.; Leiden: Brill, 1975, 1976, 1988)).

21e *on his arrival there*: Herodotus too claims that Solon travelled to Egypt in the time of Amasis (1. 30). This is chronologically plausible, since Amasis came to the throne in 570 and Solon died about 560. But Plato has just said (21c) that Solon visited Egypt *before* his Athenian reforms, which is hardly plausible. Plato's account of Solon's activities in Egypt resembles Herodotus' account of his own activities there.

22b *he was talking about*: in Argive legend Phoroneus was an early, or even first, ancestor; his daughter Niobe was the founding mother, by Zeus, of the Argive race. The Noah-like legend of Deucalion and his wife Pyrrha has them warned by Prometheus that Zeus was going to destroy the corrupt human race; they built a boat, stocked it with provisions, and rode out the deluge. Afterwards, according to the best-known version of the myth, they were told to veil themselves and throw their mother's bones over their shoulders. They interpreted this odd command correctly: they threw stones—the bones of Mother Earth—over their shoulders, and these stones were transformed into human beings so that the earth was restocked with people. It sounds as though Solon attempted to systematize and rationalize the chaos of Greek legend in the way that several Greek proto-historians of the fifth century had done.

22d *to a real event*: so myths can be disguised truth. This, I think, is a model for how we are to take the Atlantis story. On the one hand, Plato takes pains to distinguish the Egyptian's account of the past, as true, from Greek accounts; but by drawing our attention so often to its supposed accuracy he actually reminds us to doubt it. It is in fact no more than a plausible account designed for present purposes, and is therefore true not in the sense that it describes hard historical facts, but in the sense that it is 'an illustration of a general truth' (T. K. Johansen, 'Truth, Lies and History in Plato's *Timaeus–Critias*', *Histos*, 2 (1998))—in this case how the ideally good citizens of Plato's *Republic* would behave if they were to become actual.

22d *deviation*: the same word as at *Statesman* 269e, though there the alteration of the course of the heavenly bodies is part of a myth, not a hard fact.

22d *by being released*: the Egyptians used Nile water to irrigate their land with a complex system of canals. The old priest's suggestion seems to be that releasing the river water into this network of canals keeps the land and its inhabitants from being scorched by the cosmic fire.

22e *from above*: Egyptian lack of rain was notorious.

22e *rises up from below*: the reasons for the peculiar nature of the Nile, which floods in the summer and decreases in the winter, was a source of endless speculation among Greek scientists.

23e *a thousand years later*: the antiquity and primacy of Egypt was almost universally acknowledged among the Greeks, and so this statement of the primacy of Athens is truly remarkable. In Athenian legend Erichthonius, their first ancestor, was the offspring of the deities Earth and Hephaestus (or the elements earth and fire), after Hephaestus' seed had fallen to the ground during a bungled rape of Athena.

24a *in your part of the world*: more relevant, though, than any supposed similarities with ancient Egypt, are similarities with the ideal and unrealizable constitution sketched in Plato's *Republic*.

24b *in Asia*: on the Greek division of the three recognized continents (Europe, Asia, and Libya (Africa)), with Egypt forming part of Asia, see Herodotus 2. 15–18.

24b *the example of the goddess*: Athena was traditionally armed with shield and spear.

24c *men of outstanding intelligence*: on the famed temperateness of the Athenian climate and its supposed effect on the development of intelligence, see, for instance, Euripides, *Medea* 826–9; ps.-Hippocrates, *Airs, Waters, Places* 5; Aristotle, *Politics* 1327b.

24e *Pillars of Heracles*: our Strait of Gibraltar.

25a *genuine sea*: the traditional Greek view of the world held that the three continents were surrounded by an enormous river called Oceanus. Plato adds that there is another continent, or mainland, surrounding the entire plate-like world, and that this continent, because of its size, truly deserves the name 'mainland', just as the further sea around and beyond Atlantis and the three recognized continents is the only true sea.

25b *Etruria*: strictly, central Italy, but here standing for Italy as a whole.

25b *for all to see*: what follows sounds suspiciously like a description of the Athenian position during the Persian invasions of the early fifth century. For thoughts on why Plato chose a piece of pseudo-history to praise Athens, rather than the real history of the Persian invasions, see S. Broadie, 'Theodicy and Pseudo-History in the *Timaeus*', *Oxford Studies in Ancient Philosophy*, 21 (2001), 1–28.

25d *a little below the surface*: the mud and shallow water just beyond the Pillars of Heracles was apparently a familiar phenomenon: Aristotle mentions it at *Meteorologica* 354a. According to sailors, there are still sandbars to the north of the strait to beware of.

Critia, 108e–121c

108e *nine thousand years*: actually, in *Timaeus* 23e the Egyptian priest said that Saïs and Egypt were involved in the war, and that Saïs was not founded until 8,000 years ago. Moreover, in *Timaeus* the Atlanteans conscripted plenty of troops from this side of the strait, and so the war should not simply be characterized as between those on one side of the strait and those on the other. Plato is not taking these 'historical' details too seriously. It is also worth bearing in mind right from the start that Plato never finished *Critias*, and that there are several indications that the text remained unrevised.

108e *into the ocean*: see *Timaeus* 25d, with note.

109b *no disputes involved*: in keeping with the argument of *Republic* that the gods should not be portrayed as fighting, lying, stealing, killing, etc., Plato denies traditional tales such as that Poseidon and Athena competed to gain patronage of Athens.

109c *as a shepherd does his flocks*: compare *Statesman* 271d. On the relative dates of these two dialogues, see C. J. Gill, 'Plato and Politics: The *Critias* and the *Politicus*', *Phronesis*, 24 (1979), 148–67.

109d *for courage and intelligence*: see note on *Timaeus* 24c. Courage and intelligence are peculiarly suitable for Plato's prehistorical Athens, where the two classes are the guardians (under Athena, the goddess of skill and warfare) and the craftsmen (under Hephaestus, the god of craftwork and especially metallurgy). In historical Athens the two deities shared the temple which is still perched on a low hill above the Agora, and is commonly known either as the Theseum or the Hephaesteum.

109d *born from the ground*: in Athenian legend their earliest kings (Erechtheus etc.) were semi-serpentine beings who were born from the ground. Being born from the ground also signified the proud Athenian boast that they had occupied Athens and Attica from time immemorial, without ever having been displaced by invaders.

109d *already mentioned*: at *Timaeus* 22d.

110c *peculiar to their species*: for more on Plato's alleged feminism, see especially the essays collected in N. Tuana, ed., *Feminist Interpretations of Plato* (Pennsylvania State University Press, 1994).

110c *godlike men*: the supposed founders of the city.

110d *for our imaginary guardians*: the conversation of *Critias* follows straight on from that of *Timaeus*, while at the beginning of *Timaeus* Plato refers to the conversation of *Republic* as having taken place the day before. So these are the guardians of the imaginary city of *Republic*. For a solution to a residual puzzle, see C. J. Rowe, 'Why Is the Ideal Athens of the *Timaeus–Critias* Not Ruled by Philosophers?', *Methexis*, 10 (1997), 51–7.

110e *on the left*: the idea that Attica once extended west as far as the Isthmus of Corinth was irredentist wishful thinking, but Oropus was the site of frequent border disputes between Athens and Boeotia.

110e *exempt from working the land*: as opposed to the norm in historical Athens, where citizens had a duty to double up as soldiers and where 90 per cent of them worked the land.

111b *the small islands*: quite a few of the smaller islands of the Aegean have very little topsoil, and rocks are their most common feature.

112a *in the time of Deucalion*: see *Timaeus* 22b, with note. The 'single night' of earthquakes and deluge is presumably the one mentioned at *Timaeus* 25d.

112a *opposite the Pnyx*: see Map of Athens (opposite).

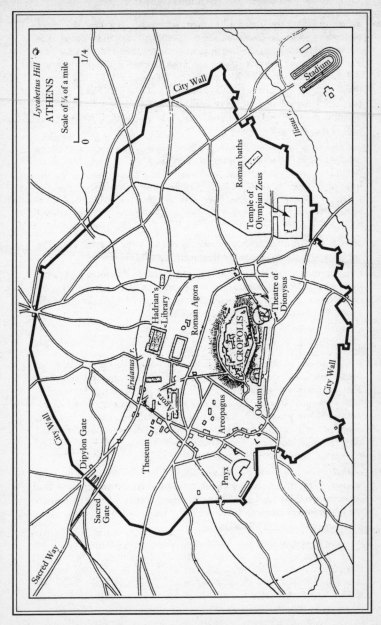

Lycabettus Hill
ATHENS
Scale of ¼ of a mile
0   ¼

City Wall

Stadium

Ilissus r.

Roman baths

Temple of
Olympian Zeus

Hadrian's
Library

Roman Agora

Theatre of
Dionysus

ACROPOLIS

Eridanus r.

Agora

Theseum

Areopagus

Odeum

City Wall

Dipylon Gate

City Wall

Pnyx

Sacred
Gate

Sacred Way

112d *willing subjects*: the pattern of their leadership was not the more oppressive Athenian empire of the fifth century, but rather the ideal of the renewed empire of the fourth century, at the time Plato was writing. For further connections between the Atlantis myth and fourth-century Athens, see the article by Morgan (n. to *Timaeus* 21a). For the general thesis that the Atlantis myth was made up by Plato partly as a 'political parable' with messages for his contemporaries, partly to reflect the ideal constitution of *Republic*, and partly as a piece of fiction, see works by Gill in the bibliography.

113b *you now know why*: since Plato himself invites us to find the names of the inhabitants of Atlantis meaningful, here is a list of their meanings: Ampheres: well made; Atlas: enduring; Autochthon: born from the ground; Azaes: enviable; Cleito: bright fame; Diaprepes: glorious; Elasippus: horse-rider; Eumelus: rich in sheep; Evaemon: of good blood; Evenor: man of courage; Leucippe: white horse; Mestor: adviser; Mneseus: rememberer.

113e *pivot of a lathe*: more precise measurements are given at 115e–116a. For the general features of the city area, see Figure 1 (opposite).

113e *been invented*: Plato leaves it ambiguous whether Poseidon is creating a utopian paradise, which was corrupted by later generations of Atlanteans, or the kind of place that would inevitably encourage the greed which would lead to the island's downfall.

114b *Gadeira*: Gadeira is modern Cadiz.

114c *as I said before*: *Timaeus* 25a–b.

114e *solid or fusible*: solid products are presumably minerals and stones, while fusible ones are all the metals. The island's rich natural resources contrast sharply not just with Plato's imaginary primeval Athens, but with historical Athens. Since all this wealth turned out to be bad for Atlantis, Plato is implicitly suggesting that Athenian austerity has been good for the city. The simplicity of primeval Athens is also contrasted with the profusion of ancient Atlantis, with its multiplicity of shrines, territories, types of building, and so on.

114e *orichalc*: 'orichalc' was a perfectly acceptable word (meaning literally 'mountain metal') in ancient Greek for copper alloys, or for the yellow copper ore used in such alloys. As such it was certainly 'more than just a name' in Plato's time, so he is using the term to refer to some more precious (and more fabulous) metal.

115b *his satiety*: several different kinds of produce are hinted at here. The 'dry' category includes 'our staple' (i.e. grain, especially barley and wheat) and pulses; the 'arboreal' sort is obviously meant to include olives and grapes (and all their derivatives), but also other fruits. We do not know what fruit was offered diners to relieve satiety—perhaps a lemon.

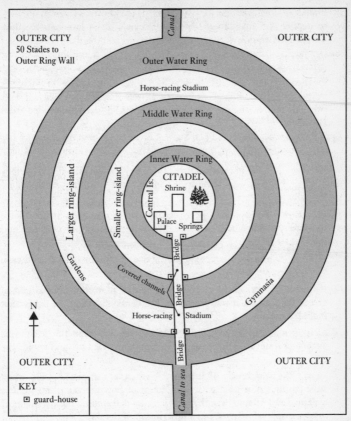

FIGURE 1. The capital city of Atlantis. After C. J. Gill, *Plato: The Atlantis Story* (Bristol Classical Press, 1980)

115d *fifty stades long*: on the Athenian scale a foot is 29.6 centimetres, a plethron is 29.6 metres, and a stade is 177.6 metres.

115e *underground sailing passage below*: it is hard to see how the struts supporting the bridges could coincide with the mouths of these underground canals, especially since in at least once instance the canal is wider than the bridge: the bridges are one plethron wide (116a) and the outermost canal is three plethra wide.

116c *which gleamed like fire*: compare Herodotus' description of the various concentric walls of Ecbatana (*Histories* 1. 98). The defensive walls of

Plato's Atlantis increase in value towards the centre: bronze is an alloy of copper and tin, and of these two metals tin is less valuable than copper (orichalc).

116d *the appearance of the temple*: it is non-Greek in its over-lavish use of precious metals and in its enormous size (three times larger than the Parthenon), but its basic design is Greek. The palace of Homer's never-never land, Phaeacia (*Odyssey* 7), was similarly embellished with precious metals, and the Phaeacian king was similarly descended from Poseidon.

116d *acroteria*: ornamental devices crowning the top or side angles of the triangular pediment of an ancient Greek temple.

116e *this many Nereids*: in classical times there were usually thought to be fifty of them. Nereids were sea-nymphs and as such they often accompanied Poseidon.

117c *bodyguards*: perhaps for the first time, a sour note is struck, since to Greek thinking bodyguards indicated tyranny rather than fair and tolerant leadership.

118b *faced south*: because there were mountains to the north, west, and east, see Figure 2 (opposite).

120b *the feast*: a large animal sacrifice was always an occasion for a feast in Greek life. In fact, it was one of the few occasions when the Greek diet included meat.

120d *the god*: it was Zeus, as we discover at 121b, who sent the Atlanteans against primeval Athens as a roundabout way of punishing the Atlanteans.

121c *he said*: the work breaks off here, and Plato never completed it. He would have continued at least with an account of how the punishment Zeus ordained for Atlantis was that it was to be defeated by the paradigm of virtue, primeval Athens, and a description of the war.

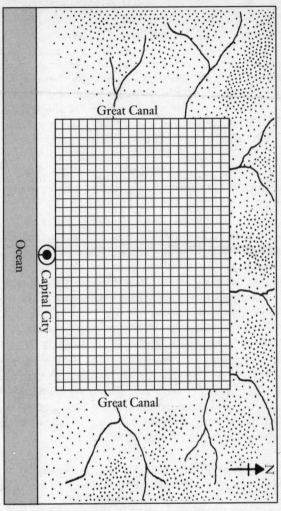

FIGURE 2. The coastal plain of Atlantis. After C. J. Gill, *Plato:
The Atlantis Story* (Bristol Classical Press, 1980)

CONTRIBUTORS

LUC BRISSON is Senior Research Fellow at the National Centre of Scientific Research (CNRS), Paris. He is author of *Plato the Myth Maker* (University of Chicago Press); he has also translated into French Plato's *Symposium*, *Parmenides*, *Phaedrus*, *Timaeus*, and *Critias* (all published by GF-Flammarion).

LESLEY BROWN is Centenary Fellow of Somerville College, Oxford. She is the author of numerous articles and book chapters on ancient philosophy.

MICHAEL CHASE is Research Engineer at the National Centre of Scientific Research (CNRS), Paris, and Associate Editor of *L'Année Philologique*. He has translated from the French Pierre Hadot's *Plotinus, or the Simplicity of Vision* (University of Chicago Press), *Philosophy as a Way of Life* (Blackwell), and *What is Ancient Philosophy?* (Harvard University Press).

JOHN DILLON is Professor of Philosophy at Trinity College Dublin. His most recent publications include *The Heirs of Plato* (Oxford University Press), and *The Great Tradition: Further Studies in the Development of Platonism and Christianity* (Ashgate). He also also translated with commentary Alcinous' *The Handbook of Platonism* (Oxford University Press). *Traditions of Platonism* (Ashgate) is a collection of essays published in his honour.

DAVID GALLOP is Professor of Philosophy (Emeritus) at Trent University, Ontario. He is the author of Plato, *Phaedo* (Clarendon Plato Series), *Parmenides of Elea* (Toronto University Press), and *Aristotle on Sleep and Dreams* (Broadview Press).

CATALIN PARTENIE is a Fellow of the University of Quebec at Montreal. He has translated into Romanian Plato's *Timaeus* (in collaboration), *Critias*, and *Menexenus*, and is co-editor of *Plato's Complete Works in Romanian* (Humanitas). He has also co-edited (with Tom Rockmore) *Heidegger and Plato* (Northwestern University Press).

ROBIN WATERFIELD has been a university lecturer (at Newcastle upon Tyne and St Andrews), and an editor and publisher. Currently, however, he is a self-employed writer, whose books range from philosophy to children's fiction. He has previously translated, for Oxford World's Classics, Plato's *Republic*, *Symposium*, *Gorgias*, and *Phaedrus*, Aristotle's *Physics*, Herodotus' *Histories*, Plutarch's *Roman Lives* and *Greek Lives*, Euripides' *Orestes and Other Plays* and *Heracles and Other Plays*, and *The First Philosophers: The Presocratics and the Sophists*.

C. C. W. TAYLOR is a Fellow of Corpus Christi College, Oxford, and Tutor in Philosophy. He is the author of *Plato*, Protagoras (Clarendon Plato Series), co-author (with J. C. B. Gosling) of *The Greeks on Pleasure* (Clarendon Press), and editor of volume i of *The Routledge History of Philosophy*.

INDEX OF NAMES

Aeacus: son of Zeus and Aegina, the eponymous nymph of the island near Athens, on which Aeacus lived. He was famous for his piety, for being Achilles' grandfather, and for becoming one of the judges of the underworld. Plato is the first to name these judges, at *Apology* 41a.

Aeschylus: *c.*525–456, the earliest of the three outstanding Athenian tragic playwrights; he established the basic forms of classical tragedy.

Agamemnon: the leader of the Greek army during the legendary Trojan War of the Homeric poems; son of Atreus and brother of Menelaus; he was murdered on his return from Troy by his wife Clytemnestra and her lover Aegisthus.

Agathon: born *c.*445. In his time, he was a highly regarded tragic playwright, though only a few lines of his work are extant now. He was famous as a modernizer (e.g. for not drawing his plots from myth and for not integrating his choral odes with the plots of his plays), for his somewhat overblown poetry, for his physical beauty, for his affair with PAUSANIAS, and for having been influenced by the sophistic movement. He left Athens in 407 and emigrated to the court of King Archelaus of Macedon, who was a great patron of the arts.

Aphrodite: the goddess of attraction and sexual love (originally of fertility); married to HEPHAESTUS and lover of ARES.

Apollo: god of disease, medicine, music, reason, civilization, and prophecy. Delphi, in the district of Pytho, was sacred to him as the god of prophecy.

Archelaus: king of Macedon 413–399 BCE. He continued the unifying work of his predecessor Perdiccas II, and was also famous as a patron of the arts: Euripides and Agathon, the tragedians, accepted invitations to his court, for instance. He apparently also issued such an invitation to Socrates, but Socrates refused. He was, at least for a while, a valued ally of Athens. In painting him as the type of immorality, then, Plato is justifying Socrates' judgement over that of Athens.

Ardiaeus: a fictional character in 'Er's Journey into the Other World', who was supposed to be a dictator in Pamphylia (a region occupying part of the coast of what is now Turkey, north-west of Cyprus).

Ares: the god of the frenzy of war. He fell for APHRODITE's charms and they had a notorious affair which ended when Aphrodite's husband HEPHAESTUS ensnared them *in flagrante delicto* in a magic net he had made and summoned all the rest of the gods to come and look.

Aristophanes: *c.*450–*c.*385. The greatest playwright of Athenian Old Comedy, notorious for its slapstick obsessions with sex, food, alcohol, farting, and belching. It was also a powerful tool of social and political satire—

no public figure was safe (Socrates himself is unfairly parodied in the *Clouds*, as is AGATHON in *Thesmophoriazousae*). His speech in *Symposium* approximates to his plays only in the element of the fantastic.

Atalanta: mythical female athlete; like Artemis, she enjoyed hunting and virginity; she was so sure of her abilities that she promised to marry anyone who could beat her in a race, but the cunning Hippomenes slowed her down by dropping golden apples, which she could not resist.

Athena: the patron goddess of Athens, and the goddess of skill at war and of traditionally female skills, especially weaving.

Atreus: accursed father of Agamemnon and Menelaus; see note to *Statesman* 268e (p. 146).

Atropos: one of the three Fates; her name means 'implacable'.

Callicles: unknown outside *Gorgias*, but surely a historical person, rather than a Platonic fiction, since Plato tells us about his love for Demus (481d–e, 513b), and names his deme (495d) and three of his friends (487c). He may well have died young, and therefore left no further traces in the historical record. Nevertheless, Plato uses him as a type: he is a conventionally educated young Athenian aristocrat who has been influenced enough by the new ideas current at the end of the fifth century to be a spokesman for a materialistic and hedonistic personal philosophy.

Cebes: see SIMMIAS OF THEBES.

Clotho: one of the three Fates; her name means 'weaver' and she was supposed to weave the threads of a person's life.

Critias: *c.*460–403, an Athenian, first cousin of Plato's mother. An associate of Alcibiades, he was opposed to the Athenian democracy, and was one of the most extreme among the Thirty Tyrants, the oppressive dictatorship which seized power in Athens from 404 to 403. He was killed in the fighting which accompanied the overthrow of the tyranny. He was a poet, dramatist, and prose writer, of whose works some fragments survive (DK 88). He has a prominent part in the *Charmides* (one of Plato's early dialogues, named after Charmides of Athens, Plato's uncle and a member of Socrates' circle).

Cronus: father of Zeus and chief deity before Zeus took over; Zeus raised an army of horrendous giants etc. to defeat Cronus and his fellow Titans and imprison them in Tartarus; the best account is in Hesiod (*Theogony* 453–885).

Diotima: though the name is attested elsewhere, she is probably a fiction of Plato for the purpose of the dialogue. Even if she is, or is based on, a historical figure, she has become in the dialogue a mouthpiece for Platonic doctrine. As such, she allows Socrates to show up the superficiality of his friends' speeches in a polite manner appropriate to the context, and to exhibit his question-and-answer technique while pretending to obey the rules of the contest and give a speech. Since there is a delicious ambiguity whether the *intellectual* side of Love's mysteries is all that she initiated Socrates into, it is tempting to see her as one of those educated courtesans whose prime historical example is Aspasia (common-law wife of Pericles).

Her primary model, however, is that of the itinerant mystic: see note on *Symposium* 201d (p. 127).

Ephialtes: a giant in mythology who, with his companion Otus, was notoriously hostile to the rule of the Olympic pantheon. Their most famous escapade was to launch an attack on heaven by piling Mount Ossa on top of Mount Olympus (high above which was the abode of the gods), and then Pelion on top of Ossa.

Epimetheus: the son of Iapetus and Clymene, and brother of PROMETHEUS.

Er: the fictitious subject of the extremely vivid near-death experience with which Plato concludes *Republic*. His name is meant to suggest the Middle East; his father's name—Armenius—is reminiscent of Armenia; and Er is said to come from Pamphylia (see ARDIAEUS).

Eros: the Greek god of love and sexual desire. One of the oldest gods; according to one genealogy, he was the son of Aphrodite and Ares.

Eryximachus: one of the new professional doctors of the end of the fifth century, who was obviously well known in Athenian intellectual circles, since he crops up from time to time in other Socratic writings of Plato and Xenophon.

Fates: the goddesses who controlled the destiny of each human being, from birth to death. They are CLOTHO, LACHESIS, and ATROPOS. Although immortal, even gods fear them.

Ganymede: a good-looking legendary prince of Troy with whom Zeus fell in love. In his only act of homosexual seduction (compared to his many heterosexual affairs), Zeus took him away to Olympus to act as cup-bearer to the gods.

Glaucon: brother of Plato and Adeimantus; one of the two secondary interlocutors of *Republic*.

Gorgias: *c.*480–376, from Leontini in Sicily; one of the giants of the sophistic movement, and a well-known figure in Athens. He specialized not in philosophy, but in the budding art of rhetoric, in which he was a great innovator; although much of his style seems horribly artificial to us today, it seems to have dazzled his contemporaries. 'Starting with the initial advantage of having nothing in particular to say, he was able to concentrate all his energies upon saying it' (J. D. Denniston, *Greek Prose Style* (London: Oxford University Press, 1952), 12).

Hades: see PLUTO.

Hephaestus: the lame smith of the Olympic pantheon (originally with all the magical connotations that accrue to smiths the world over). In one tradition, mankind was his creation: this, as well as his role as metal-worker, probably underlies his role in ARISTOPHANES' speech at *Symposium* 192d–e.

Hermes: god of communication, heralds, magic, and wayfarers.

Hesiod: fl. *c.*700; after Homer, considered the second greatest epic poet of Greece; his *Theogony* orders the gods into rationalistic genealogies and recounts stories about many of them, while *Works and Days* is full of practical and moral advice for rural daily life.

Homer: fl. *c.*750 BCE. The greatest epic poet of Greece; his *Iliad* sings of the death and glory of the Trojan War, while his *Odyssey* recounts the fanciful and marvellous adventures of one hero, Odysseus, returning from the war.

Lachesis: one of the three Fates; her name means 'she who allots'.

Minos: legendary king of Crete, and builder of the labyrinth. The son of Zeus and Europa, he was credited with establishing a good legal code in Crete, which is presumably what entitles him to become a judge in the underworld. One of the other judges, Rhadamanthys, was his brother.

Niobe: in Greek myth the archetype of grief; she boasted that, because she had borne twelve children, she was better than Leto, who had only borne two; but those two were the deities Apollo and Artemis, who then killed all her children; in her grief Niobe was turned into a weeping rock, which was a famous spectacle.

Oceanus: the personification of the ocean. Son of Uranus and Gaia, and father of all rivers.

Odysseus: the resourceful hero of Homer's *Iliad* and (especially) *Odyssey*, which tells the stories of his arduous journey home from the Trojan War, plagued by the hatred of the god POSEIDON.

Otus: see EPHIALTES.

Pausanias: scarcely known apart from *Symposium*, and chiefly known as AGATHON's lover. This probably explains his entry into this dialogue, where he is the champion of homosexuality—a rather outspoken champion, to judge by Xenophon's criticism in his own *Symposium* (8. 32–4).

Phaedo: a close friend of Socrates, from Elis in the Peloponnese. Little is known of him beyond what can be gathered from the *Phaedo* dialogue. According to Diogenes Laertius (philosophical biographer of the third century CE), he was taken captive by the Athenians, was ransomed at the instance of Socrates, and thereafter practised philosophy 'as a free man' (*Lives of the Philosophers*, 2. 105). It is not known why the dialogue is named after him, but possibly it was he who gave the original, first-hand account of Socrates' death to Plato himself.

Phaedrus: *c.*450–390. Phaedrus is mentioned briefly in Plato's *Protagoras*, but figures prominently in *Symposium*, where he gives the first speech about love. He was exiled from Athens in 415, when he was caught up in the scandal, which also brought down Alcibiades, surrounding the mutilation of the Herms just before the vast Athenian expedition set sail for Sicily. Herms were busts of Hermes on top of square-cut blocks of stone, set up at road junctions in Athens. They had erect phalluses, and on one night they all had their phalluses broken off, and were otherwise mutilated. Phaedrus returned to Athens after the end of the war, when a general amnesty was declared.

Phaethon: son of Helios (the personification of the sun). One day Helios allowed him to drive the chariot of the sun across the sky; the horses ran wildly and Zeus, fearing the chariot might burn the earth, destroyed Phaethon with a thunderbolt.

Pluto: also known as Hades or Dis. Brother of Zeus and Poseidon, in a tripartite world he gained the underworld as his domain, while Zeus took the upper air and Poseidon the surface of the earth.

Polus: from Acragas in Sicily, a pupil of Gorgias, and imitator of his rhetorical techniques. He was the author of a handbook on rhetoric, and a professional teacher of the subject. Plato's portrait of him is severe: he is rude and unintelligent. Callicles' robust self-reliance would almost have seemed attractive to Plato, especially in his youth, if it were not so arrogant; but there is little attractive about Polus' superficial ideas, though Plato may well have taken them to be typical of his times.

Poseidon: brother of Zeus and Pluto, and lord of the surface of the earth (hence mainly of the sea), as Zeus is of the upper air and Pluto is of the underworld.

Prometheus: his name means 'foresight', which perhaps explains why Zeus used him as he did at *Gorgias* 523d–e: since foresight is his domain, he deprived humans of their foreknowledge of their death, so that it always comes as a surprise. More generally, he is seen in Greek myth as a benefactor of humanity, especially by providing them with the civilizing and evolutionary knowledge of fire.

Protagoras: *c.*490–420, from Abdera, on the north coast of the Aegean. The first professional sophist, i.e. itinerant professor of higher education. He had a long and successful career, travelling widely throughout the Greek world and making very large sums of money. He aimed to teach upper-class youths how to attain personal and political success, putting considerable emphasis on skill in speech and argument, in which he developed a systematic method of teaching. He is said to have written a number of works in this area, and on more general ethical and philosophical topics. A few quotations are preserved, expressing agnosticism on the existence of the gods and extreme subjectivism, according to which every belief is true for the person who holds it. The latter position is criticized at length by Plato in *Theaetetus*.

Rhadamanthys: brother of MINOS. Little legend accrued to him, apart from his being just and hence becoming one of the judges in the underworld.

Simmias of Thebes: Thebes was the chief city in Boeotia, about sixty kilometres north-west of Athens. Simmias and Cebes are mentioned in *Crito* (45b), as having brought money to procure Socrates' escape from gaol.

Sirens: although in Homer they were wicked women whose charming singing lured sailors to their death, by Plato's time they were well on their way (largely through Pythagorean influence) to becoming virtual demigods of song, and singers of universal harmony.

Sisyphus: one of the great sinners of Greek myth, though details of his crime against Zeus are unclear. His punishment was to roll a stone up a hill, which then rolled back down and he had to start all over again.

Socrates: 469–399 BCE. Born in Athens, where he spent all his life, apart from periods of military service, engaged in the informal discussion of philosophical (mainly ethical) topics. Though he never engaged in formal teaching, he gathered round himself a circle of mainly younger men, including Plato, many of whom were opposed to the extreme form of democracy current in Athens. He was put to death on vague charges of impiety and corruption of youth, which were probably politically inspired. His philosophical views and methods were a major influence on Plato, but the ascription of any specific doctrine to Socrates is a matter of much controversy. He wrote nothing himself, but in the fourth century many accounts of his personality and teaching were written, mostly friendly, but some hostile, with different degrees of approximation to historical truth. The most substantial element of this literature to survive is in the dialogues of Plato; Socrates also figures in a number of works by Xenophon. The *Clouds* of Aristophanes, first produced in 423, gives a contemporary caricature.

Solon: fl. *c.*590, Athenian statesman and lyric poet; one of the constant members of the varying lists of seven sages of Greece; considered in Athenian popular history as the founding father of democracy in Athens.

Tantalus: perhaps the most famous of the great sinners of Greek myth. Of the several versions of his story, the best-known has him standing in a pool of water, with a fruit-laden tree above him. Every time he bends down for a drink, the water recedes; every time he reaches up for some food, the branches withdraw. This was punishment to fit the crime, because he had killed and cooked his son Pelops and served him up to the gods to see if they could tell.

Thersites: the only non-aristocrat to have a speaking part in Homer's *Iliad* (2. 212 ff.); it is not a favourable part, however, and to later ages he was the archetype of the buffoon or villain.

Theseus: son of POSEIDON; legendary early king, and national hero, of Athens; a great many tales were told about his various adventures.

Timaeus: active in the latter half of the fifth century BCE. Astronomer and philosopher, he was elected to high office in Locri. Unknown outside Plato's *Timaeus* and *Critias*.

Tityus: for attempting to rape the Titan Leto, he was punished in Hades by being spreadeagled on the ground and having vultures rip out his liver (which was seen as the seat of desire). Each night the liver grew again, ready for the vultures the next day.

Young Socrates: of Athens. He is present in *Theaetetus* (147c) and *Sophist* (218b), and he is the interlocutor of the Stranger from Elea in *Statesman*. 'I have no reason whatever to think this is a fabricated character or a stand-in for someone else' (D. Nails, *The People of Plato* (Indianapolis:

Hackett, 2002), 269). The name 'Socrates', however, was common and we cannot be sure who 'young Socrates' might have been.

Zeus: king of the gods. As the most elevated of the gods, he is taken by Plato to be the appropriate god for philosophers.

For information on others appearing or mentioned in the ten myths collected here, see Explanatory Notes. For more information on the characters appearing or mentioned in Plato's dialogues see D. Nails, *The People of Plato: A Prosopography of Plato and Other Socratics* (Indianapolis: Hackett, 2002). For more information on the deities appearing or mentioned in Plato's dialogues see M. Grant and J. Hazel, *Who's Who in Classical Mythology* (Oxford: Oxford University Press, 1993).

	Classical Literary Criticism
	The First Philosophers: The Presocratics and the Sophists
	Greek Lyric Poetry
	Myths from Mesopotamia
APOLLODORUS	The Library of Greek Mythology
APOLLONIUS OF RHODES	Jason and the Golden Fleece
APULEIUS	The Golden Ass
ARISTOPHANES	Birds and Other Plays
ARISTOTLE	The Nicomachean Ethics
	Physics
	Politics
BOETHIUS	The Consolation of Philosophy
CAESAR	The Civil War
	The Gallic War
CATULLUS	The Poems of Catullus
CICERO	Defence Speeches
	The Nature of the Gods
	On Obligations
	The Republic and The Laws
EURIPIDES	Bacchae and Other Plays
	Medea and Other Plays
	Orestes and Other Plays
	The Trojan Women and Other Plays
GALEN	Selected Works
HERODOTUS	The Histories
HOMER	The Iliad
	The Odyssey

The Oxford World's Classics Website

www.worldsclassics.co.uk

- Information about new titles
- Explore the full range of Oxford World's Classics
- Links to other literary sites and the main OUP webpage
- Imaginative competitions, with bookish prizes
- Peruse the Oxford World's Classics Magazine
- Articles by editors
- Extracts from Introductions
- A forum for discussion and feedback on the series
- Special information for teachers and lecturers

www.worldsclassics.co.uk

American Literature

British and Irish Literature

Children's Literature

Classics and Ancient Literature

Colonial Literature

Eastern Literature

European Literature

History

Medieval Literature

Oxford English Drama

Poetry

Philosophy

Politics

Religion

The Oxford Shakespeare

A complete list of Oxford Paperbacks, including Oxford World's Classics, Oxford Shakespeare, Oxford Drama, and Oxford Paperback Reference, is available in the UK from the Academic Division Publicity Department, Oxford University Press, Great Clarendon Street, Oxford OX2 6DP.

In the USA, complete lists are available from the Paperbacks Marketing Manager, Oxford University Press, 198 Madison Avenue, New York, NY 10016.

Oxford Paperbacks are available from all good bookshops. In case of difficulty, customers in the UK can order direct from Oxford University Press Bookshop, Freepost, 116 High Street, Oxford OX1 4BR, enclosing full payment. Please add 10 per cent of published price for postage and packing.